About the Author

Angela Primachenko loves her husband and two girls more than anything in the world. She is a respiratory therapist with additional credentials as a neonatal pediatric specialist. She has one goal in life: to love well and hope that, in some small way, her life can bring someone closer to Jesus.

Breath of Life

Angela Primachenko

Breath of Life

Olympia Publishers
London

www.olympiapublishers.com
OLYMPIA PAPERBACK EDITION

A CIP catalogue record for this title is
available from the British Library.

ISBN: 978-1-80074-878-1

First Published in 2023

Olympia Publishers
Tallis House
2 Tallis Street
London
EC4Y 0AB

Printed in Great Britain

Dedication

This book would not be possible without an amazing, supportive team and lovely friends. I am forever grateful. Dedicated to my amazing husband, David, my Medvedev and Primachenko family, my incredible friends, and all the staff at Legacy Health.

Acknowledgments

A huge thank you to Ang Riesterer, Nadia Kashitskaya, and therapist and workbook consultant, Anastasia Ethridge.

ONE

It was a typical March afternoon in the Pacific Northwest. The months of nonstop rain were coming to an end, and spring was right around the corner. As I walked along a trail near my house in Vancouver, Washington, I could almost feel the coming days when the sunshine basked you with warmth and…oh no, here it comes—*achuuuu*!—oh, allergies. Ahh, those allergies seemed to creep up on me every year. I stopped to catch my breath, feeling the little kicks in my belly reminding me to slow down.

I was a respiratory therapist, thirty-one weeks into my second pregnancy with another little girl. On top of my work at a local hospital, constantly chasing my ten-month-old daughter around and those persistent allergies, I was exhausted by the end of the day. I knew it was typical for symptoms to vary from pregnancy to pregnancy, but this one was wiping me out. Aches and pains I was too distracted to notice during the day were very pronounced at night. It felt like darts were shooting through my body; my head hurt, my lungs ached and my heart rate seemed to be getting faster and faster. As the baby grew and took up more room, I noticed it was getting more difficult to breathe.

"When do allergies normally start going away?" I asked my friend, Abby, impatiently.

"Maybe you have the coronavirus," Abby joked.

"No way—that's something only older people get," I responded, rolling my eyes. "And besides, there haven't been any known cases in our area."

The only coronavirus cases I was aware of were on the opposite side of the globe. At this point in the COVID-19 pandemic, we were still living our normal lives; restaurants and public places were still open and no one was wearing a face mask.

Unfortunately, those sneezes—which ended up not being caused by allergies but by something far more sinister—started hurting my lungs more and more. I was feeling increasingly tired, but I comforted myself with the thought that anyone would be exhausted with a ten-month-old at home and a thirty-one-week-old growing inside of them. So just like countless other moms, I kept pushing along, resting when I could, but staying busy caring for my family and home.

A few days later, Emmie, my older daughter, felt a little heavier and my lungs a little more worn out. *Could it be a cold?* I thought to myself. My husband, David, came home from work and after hearing my two-minute coughing session, asked if I needed to go to the hospital. But that was David, always suggesting I go to the hospital for every little thing. A splinter. Sore muscles after working out. It felt like another day, another joke. "No, babe, I'm fine," I said, smiling at him. Having worked in an emergency department for three years, I learned a lot, and I refused to be "that" patient—the one that overthinks and overreacts.

However, as the day went on, I realized I was starting to feel increasingly weak. *I'll check my temp*, I thought, *maybe I have a cold.* Sure enough, my temperature was elevated to 102.8 degrees Fahrenheit. *All right, I guess there's no harm in taking it easy for the next few days.* I still refused to make a big deal about it. After all, everyone gets sick occasionally, and most of the time it's nothing to worry about. I believed I would be fine; I wasn't concerned.

As the day drew to a close, it felt like my heart was beating a little faster. By the time evening rolled around, I had had a long and productive day, but I was very tired and couldn't get comfortable. With both pregnancies, one of my ribs annoyingly popped out of place. I've been told it's a natural occurrence—an increase in hormones loosens my joints to help prepare my body for labor. But it sure was painful. That night, I kept hearing and feeling the rib clicking in and out of place, sending shooting pain along my rib cage. I couldn't find a comfortable position lying down that didn't send me into a coughing spasm. I kept thinking, *tomorrow I'll feel better*, desperately trying to squeeze in even a minute of sleep.

But the next day wasn't better. The thermometer read 103 when I took my temperature and my heart raced 120 beats a minute. I called my mom, who thankfully lives nearby, and she insisted that she would take Emmie so I could get more rest.

I had gone to my bedroom to try and get ready for the day, but yet another coughing session interrupted my plans. I was sitting on my bed, sweaty and gross, when my parents walked in. "Mom, Dad, what are you doing here?" I asked.

"David called us and we are going to anoint you with anointing oil," was their loving and faith-filled response. They prayed over me. I appreciated the prayer and felt so much peace, completely unaware of the risk my parents were in, just by being in the same room as me.

My parents took Emmie to their house and as I watched them drive away, I had no idea that I wouldn't see her again for almost a month.

Once again, the night was hard. So hard in fact, that I finally caved and decided it wouldn't hurt to get seen by a provider. I was thirty-two weeks pregnant at this point and thought perhaps there was something I could take to bring relief. Unfortunately, it was the weekend and my usual doctor's office was closed, so I had to go to the emergency department. News of the coronavirus was now gaining significant attention, but Washington State had not yet mandated masking, and I saw few people wearing masks in public. The hospital no longer allowed visitors to come into the emergency department with patients, so David dropped me off and drove away. I didn't feel lonely or even scared; I knew I would be fine and was confident that they would let me go home that same day. *Just give me a treatment or a prescription for medication and I can be on my jolly way.*

A sense of familiarity filled me as I entered the hospital—it was the same place I had worked in for almost eight years, first as an operating room tech, then an emergency room tech, and now as a respiratory therapist. Coworkers I recognized quickly helped me, took my vitals, and got me into a room. I thought to myself, *I'm probably overreacting... but I'm pregnant, so guess it can't hurt to get checked out.* David's persistence was getting to me; his nonstop comments of "You should go get seen" had hit their mark. Knowing that I would be getting checked out by doctors reassured me that everything was going to be OK. I had no clue about the danger my health and my baby's health were in.

But my heart was beating a little bit faster than I would have liked, and my temperature just wouldn't go down. I remained hopeful that I would feel better after I got some IV fluids. At this point, there was no rapid testing for the coronavirus. The only testing being done was the nasal swab, which took twenty-four to seventy-two hours to produce results. The swab was so uncomfortable; it felt like they were flossing my brain.

It didn't take long before the emergency department doctor

came back and said that my chest X-ray looked as if I might indeed have the coronavirus. I literally laughed out loud when she said that. "Coronavirus? No way, that's something only older people get." The doctor continued to tell me that there was not much they could do for me at the time, since it was a virus. I could leave, and if I got significantly worse, then I should come back. *What does "significantly worse" mean?* I already felt pretty terrible. How much worse could I—or would I— get? But I was happy that I was being discharged home. I could finally tell David that all of his worries were for nothing.

CHAPTER ONE – QUESTIONS

Living in a culture of never-ending hurry, we often don't take the time to listen to our bodies or emotions. We simply press through, keeping busy. Even worse, we often use busyness to avoid dealing with hard emotions. When facing a difficult emotion, we can often explode, shut down or go numb.

I remember trying to get my nails done one day and being so frustrated that the nail technician was running late. That would add more hurrying to my already busy day, and it's frustrating to lose control of my time. But why? Why can't I just go with the flow?

There are many situations that are out of our control. However, we do have control over emotions. There are healthy and unhealthy ways of coping with emotions and stress.

1.) What are three unhealthy ways that you tend to cope with stress? (E.g., alcohol, keeping busy, TV, social media, porn, stress eating, ignoring your emotions, pushing through, etc.) If you are unaware of your negative coping methods, ask your close friends or loved ones, they may have some insight.

....
....
....
....

2.) What are three healthy, alternative coping methods you have used to help you deal with your emotions? (E.g., exercising, talking it through with a close trusted friend, spending time with the Lord, finding supportive scripture to stand on, worshipping, walking, etc.)

....

....

....

....

3.) Name three things that God is telling you to do in this season. It's important to be aware of the things that God has placed on your heart to do. When we do His work, He will give us grace for it. However, if we feel burned out or stressed, are we confident that we are doing what God is requesting of us?

....

....

....

....

4.) What are three things you have placed on yourself that might *not* have been God's guidance? There are some things that we add to our plate that God is not asking us to do. Are there things on your plate that you can delegate to someone else, or is there an area in your life that you can get help in? (E.g., hiring a babysitter, being OK with a messy house, suggesting someone else lead the group, etc.)

....

....

....
....

5.) How do you spend your down/alone time? I often felt
that when I would have alone time, instead of addressing
my emotions, I would try to stay busy (e.g., scrolling
through Instagram, calling a friend, keeping busy with
house chores, etc.) This was because I simply didn't
have the emotional strength to deal with hard topics.
....
....
....
....

6.) What are things you can do to help you feel relaxed
and recharged? As a mom, I have very little alone time.
When I feel overwhelmed, I play worship music or even
take thirty seconds and walk into another room just to
regain my composure.
....
....
....
....

7.) What does Jesus say about rest? God Himself worked
six days and rested on the seventh day, providing us with
an example to follow. Being at rest doesn't mean we
neglect to work, we simply need to be aware of the
importance of rest.
....
....

SCRIPTURES

Hebrews 4:10: "For all who have entered into God's rest have rested from their labors, just as God did after creating the world."

Psalm 91:1: "Those who live in the shelter of the Most High will find rest in the shadow of the Almighty."

Jeremiah 31:15: "For I have given rest to the weary and joy to the sorrowing."

Psalm 127:2: "It is useless for you to work so hard from early morning until late at night, anxiously working for food to eat; For God give rest to his loved ones."

TWO

Coming home from the hospital that day, I didn't feel any worse—but also not any better. I was on night four without sleep. As was now the norm, I tossed and turned all night trying to find a comfortable spot for my expanding belly where my ribs did not hurt too much and my lungs were not forced into a coughing spree.

Eating wasn't going well either. Food didn't interest me; actually, not much interested me at that point. To top it off, I began to notice that David was avoiding me. He would bring me water and would leave the room as quickly as possible. No more kisses, no more hugs. "Babe, why are you avoiding me?" I asked. He looked at me and I could tell he was trying to be nice but also honest at the same time.

"Have you seen yourself? You look so sick. I don't want to catch what you have, babe," he said. I laughed out loud, causing a coughing attack and ruining my entire appearance.

Once I regained my composure, I smirked at him, "Oh yeah? If that's true, then why are you sleeping in the same bed as me, just two feet away, eight hours every night, but then avoiding me during the day?" I smiled triumphantly. Sometimes this man's logic made no sense to me. But he continued practicing daytime social distancing before it was actually a thing. He didn't even know he would be part of a trend.

Evening came and my temperature remained high (103), and I could feel that I was growing weaker. Maybe I was now "significantly worse"? I called my doctor's office and explained that I didn't like the idea of having such a high fever and that I was starting to feel very weak. The nurse advised me to go back to the hospital. It took me a little while to get ready, seeing as every movement was a drain on my strength. I barely had the strength to do even the most basic of things, like getting ready to leave the house.

David once again dropped me off at the hospital doors. This time, a part of me wished he could stay with me. My fearless bravery seemed to be fading. I brushed it off—convincing myself I could do this—and gave David a high-five (yes, he was keeping to his daytime social distancing).

The idea of walking sounded absolutely exhausting so I happily said yes when they asked if I wanted to be wheeled to my ER room. The room felt a little lonely, but I ignored the feeling as a kind nurse came in and changed the atmosphere. This time, every nurse came in wearing a mask and it made the interaction with the staff feel a little colder. The nurse took my vitals, drew some blood, and left the room. The minutes on the clock began to drag and this inner battle arose: *Should I tell my family that I was in the ED?* I didn't want to worry anyone so instead, I picked up my phone and texted David pointless texts just to make the day go by faster.

After what felt like hours, a nurse came in. She was assigned as my "baby" nurse. She placed a monitor over my belly to catch the baby's heartbeat. At this point, we had not yet decided on a name for our baby. All we knew was that we were having a girl, but David and I just couldn't agree on a name. Little did I know that I wouldn't even be conscious to name her and that the duty would fall to David. *Swoosh swoosh. Swoosh swoosh.* I could hear my little girl's heartbeat and I let out my breath, unaware

21

that I had been holding it in anticipation. Shelly, the nurse, smiled at me and said, "She sounds amazing." I felt like I could finally relax and proceeded to lie back on the stretcher. My baby was doing well, this was *such* good news! My biggest concern was that being sick would negatively affect my daughter in some way.

I didn't know if I was supposed to be wearing a mask or not, so out of respect, I put one on anytime someone came into the room. The mask made me feel even hotter than I already was due to my fever, so the nurses constantly brought me ice packs. And I continued to wait.

Finally, the doctor came in, but he seemed preoccupied, maybe even a little careless. I had worked with him previously as a respiratory therapist but he didn't seem to recognize me. Maybe it was my mask. I sat up in the bed and smiled, hoping he would recognize my eyes, and tried to hide some of the nervousness I was feeling.

He glanced at my chart and said, "So it looks like we are going to send you home."

"Oh OK," I said, exhaling.

He looked up from his computer for half a second, our eyes met and then he looked back down at the computer screen. "Actually, I guess we could do an X-ray…oh, did you already have one? Oh, yeah, I guess you did. Yeah, I think we are going to send you home."

I replied, "Oh OK. Is there anything I can do in the meantime?"

He answered, "No, there's not much. We are still waiting on your coronavirus results. In the meantime, just stay hydrated and you can go home. The nurse will be in in a little while to give you your discharge papers and take out the IV from your arm."

"OK, thank you," I replied. He smiled at me and walked out

of the room.

I wasn't offended by his behavior because I knew exactly what it was like to be on the other side of the chart. Having worked in the emergency department, I knew he was most likely rushing to the next patient. He probably had a critical person to attend to and needed to empty my room for the next patient. I understood the necessary balance between being kind, but also efficient. Overall, healthcare professionals have a lot on their plates, so I didn't dwell on his behavior. I was just excited to get to go home. I texted David eagerly, "They are going to send me home! Told you I was fine. Lol. I'll text you once they get the IV out, for you to come get me."

I waited a while, but still, the nurse didn't come in. I kept shifting from side to side, trying to find a comfortable spot. I was still lying on the stretcher, excitedly anticipating going back to my own bed where I had five pillows that I could arrange around my large belly. Lying and waiting, I let my thoughts drift to that glorious moment when I would feel better and David would finally kiss me again. I turned my head and spotted my OB doctor, Suzanna Slayton-Mylem, walking by my room. She stopped and waved at me. *How odd that my baby's doctor is down in the ER*, I thought. A little puzzled, I continued to wait, thinking perhaps it was just a coincidence. Another twenty minutes passed and I saw Dr. Slayton-Mylem at my window, getting ready to come into my room. This time, however, instead of a simple mask like everyone else had been wearing, she was gearing up with the full spread of personal protective equipment: a helmet, gown, gloves, shoe covers, and mask. Suddenly, I was alert. The hazy tiredness I had been feeling quickly disappeared as I watched her gown up.

"Hi, honey," she greeted me as she walked in, and I could

tell she was fully present. Unlike the previous doctor, her attention and time were focused solely on me. She always amazed me with the motherly comfort she exuded. At this point in my pregnancy, I had seen her maybe six or seven times for regular prenatal check-ups. I smiled at her and placed my mask back over my face.

"Hi," I responded. "They are sending me home; I'm just waiting on the nurse to take this IV out."

She smiled and sat down next to me. "I'm sorry to say this, but your test results just came back, and you do have the coronavirus. Due to you being so weak and your fever spiking, as well as your heart rate being so elevated, I would really like for you to spend the night here at the hospital, where we can better monitor you and your baby."

I was a little taken aback by the turn of events, but readily agreed to stay at the hospital. It turns out that when I had called the advice nurse, she had told Dr. Slayton-Mylem that I was going to go to the emergency room to get checked out. Dr. Slayton-Mylem had read the ER doctor's notes stating that he was planning to discharge me, so she left her clinic and headed straight to the emergency department where she proceeded to take over my care. Her intuition and medical prowess helped save my life.

I got my phone and called David. "They changed their mind," I told him, explaining that I was going to stay there overnight. Little did I know this would be the first of twenty-one nights I spent away from him at the hospital.

I was the first pregnant patient who tested positive for coronavirus at that hospital. Protocols were still being developed, so to protect all the other expectant women who were admitted, they cleared out the entire hallway and placed me in a private wing of the family birth unit. I was starting to feel like I had some sort of plague. The nurses all wore so much PPE that it was hard to tell who was who anymore. They all just looked like yellow mushrooms. Maybe minions, depending on if they wore glasses.

I was so thirsty, but constantly coughing. It felt like my lungs were being cut by tiny blades. Every breath was excruciatingly painful. Coughing affected every muscle in my body: my back, diaphragm, and stomach all ached from the toll of each coughing fit. It felt as if the fever and all the aches took over every inch of my body.

The one thing that gave me constant comfort was the swooshing sound of my baby girl's heartbeat. The monitor they had over my belly would occasionally slip off and the nurses would have to do the entire PPE procedure before entering my room. The entire yellow mushroom ensemble came on just to readjust the monitor or to give me more water. I thought about how nice it would be to have a single family member with me— getting me a cup of water, fluffing my pillow, helping me get to the restroom. Feelings of guilt would wash over me every time a nurse would need to gown up for such a small task.

The following day felt like it dragged on forever. The nurses were trying to limit their exposure in my room. So I remained alone, trying desperately to find a comfortable position. I would try to FaceTime David or a family member, but talking would put me into another coughing session for which I didn't have the strength. I longed so deeply to have someone hold my hand or just be there. But instead, I was all alone day and night.

And my breathing was starting to get worse. I could feel the amount of effort increasing every time I took a breath. I had never thought about breathing before, but that day it was almost all I thought about. Every laborious breath. I could feel the extra energy my diaphragm required to expand and my back muscles stretching as the air staggered in and out. I felt every cough as it sent shooting pain along my back; my abs were sore, and all I wanted to do was rest. But the moment I would get comfortable, my baby would move and then the process would start all over to find that sweet spot. I wished David was with me. Here, I found myself talking to God more and more. Interestingly, I didn't beg Him to save me, it was as though I knew I would be OK. I simply thanked Him that He had given me the strength to keep going. I knew I couldn't let my thoughts go into the dark place of fear because my baby girl needed me to keep going. So, I would push aside any and every thought of that sort and keep going forward.

My lungs couldn't keep up with the energy needed to breathe, so they placed me on oxygen support. A few liters of oxygen into the nasal cannula wasn't a big deal. I remember them coming in and drawing blood to see if I was getting worse. My blood was thicker than normal and more of a deep red color. The results came back saying that I was indeed getting worse, so they placed me on a more effective oxygenation device called a high-flow nasal cannula. It was time to oxygenate my lungs more efficiently. I tried to call David after the high-flow oxygen started, but I couldn't. Pure exhaustion spread throughout my body. It was as if I had just completed the hardest workout of my life.

I was now thirty-three weeks pregnant, alone in the hospital, and diagnosed with a serious virus that no one had any effective treatment for. I remember the nurses increasing the oxygen flow and my nose feeling so dry. I wasn't even aware of how long I had been lying there anymore; my sole focus now remained on my next inhale.

Chapter Two – Questions

Coping when you are in the middle of hardship is difficult to do.

Sometimes when we are in the middle of hardship, all we can do is survive. But even then, at some point, we will need to deal with the emotions we experienced.

About four years into our marriage, we decided we wanted to have kids. I got pregnant, but miscarried our first pregnancy at eight weeks. I didn't know how to cope with that type of loss. I didn't know what to do. So, I turned on worship and invited Jesus into the pain. I wept with God, hurt and so confused. In the middle of the pain, I knew Jesus was right there with me. It was as though I was dancing in the rain. I couldn't pretend I was OK. I could feel the raindrops (the pain and hurt and disappointment) all around me. I was hurting, confused and angry. But in the middle of the pouring rain, Jesus was gently dancing with me. Filling me with hope.

Healing doesn't come from just ignoring your pain. Healing comes from partnering with what God says about your pain.

Facing your emotions is hard; however, ignoring your pain is going to bring a different set of hardships—you have the choice of which difficulties you're willing to live with. Both will have consequences: one will bring healing and the other will ultimately lead to more pain.

1.) What are things in your life that you feel you are losing control over? (E.g., children, work, finances, etc.)

....
....
....
....

2.) How are you coping with the loss of control?
....
....
....
....

3.) Are there healthier coping alternatives?
....
....
....
....

4.) Find scriptures that are directly related to what you are going through. Memorize them and speak them over your life any time those emotions arise.
....
....
....
....

5.) Talk to Jesus on a relational level and hear what He has to say about your situation and your emotions. Beyond reading the Word, it's important to understand what Jesus is directly saying to you in your unique situation. Jesus constantly reminds us throughout scripture to place our worries and burdens on Him.
....
....

....

....

SCRIPTURES

Job 23:14: "So He will do to me whatever he planned. He controls my destiny."

Proverbs 19:21: "You can make many plans, but the Lord's purpose will prevail."

Lamentations 3:37: "Who can command things to happen without the Lord's permission?"

Psalm 119:143: "As pressure and stress bear down on me, I find joy in your commands."

Philippians 4:6: "Don't worry about anything, instead pray about everything. Tell God what you need and thank Him for all that He has already done."

1 Peter 5:7: "Give all your worries and cares to God, for He cares about you."

Psalm 118:5: "In my distress, I prayed to the Lord, and the Lord answered me and set me free."

Psalm 118:6: "The Lord is for me, so I will not fear. What can mere mortals do to me?"

Proverbs 16:3: "Commit your actions to the Lord and your plans will succeed."

THREE

That day felt like a blur. I remember being in my labor and delivery room and, at some point, my oxygen saturation kept dropping. I didn't think much of it, but started to notice that it was correlating with my difficulty in breathing. Then in walked my coworker, Greg. I was hoping he was just checking in on me as a friend (and not as a patient), but the concern in Greg's eyes said it all. He was a very seasoned, exceptional critical care nurse and we had worked alongside each other many times, caring for patients. I trusted Greg and I could tell that he was very worried about me. "We are going to be moving you to the ICU," he said, words that meant my condition was only getting worse.

I was moved to the ICU and shortly after, a drug representative came in. The high-flow oxygen I was receiving made it difficult to hear, so I had to frequently ask her to repeat herself, which I could tell frustrated her. She had come to offer me an experimental drug called Remdesivir. This drug was still in the clinical trial phase for treating coronavirus, never having been tested on humans. She handed me a paper that provided statistics on her clinical trial where all the patients were rats. All I remember reading from that pamphlet was: "We have a new drug...blah blah blah...it's never been tested on humans...blah blah blah...and the rats who were given this drug survived, but they all had kidney failure." That was the summary of the pamphlet. *Oh OK*, I thought, *you want to offer me an experimental drug that has never been tested on humans and that* *made your test subjects—*rats*—end up with kidney failure? This is what you're offering not only to me, but also to my unborn baby? Yeah, no thanks.*

So, I said, "No, thank you." And I could tell once again she was frustrated.

"We got this drug specifically for you," she added, sounding irritated.

"Thank you?" was all that I could fathom to respond with. *I never asked you for this drug,* I thought. Then a new doctor came in, apparently to provide backup. "You really need to get this," he said. "There are very few people who qualify for this drug— they need to be pregnant," he said, waving a hand at my belly, "... with no underlying health conditions, and they have to be coronavirus positive and as sick as you are."

Oh goody. I was one of only a few people who met the criteria at this stage in the pandemic, but I did not feel comfortable subjecting myself and my unborn child to this experimental treatment that I didn't know anything about. He continued, "If it does well with you, it'll expedite the process so that we can give it to other people."

If it does well especially stood out and I politely, though firmly, declined a second time. No, my answer was no. I didn't have the strength to research this drug, so I took a picture of the pamphlet and asked David to look into it.

I certainly didn't have the strength when the drug representative woman came in again, just a short time later. I could barely hear what she was saying. The oxygen flow was turned up so high and the air was blowing into my nose so fast, that it felt like my head was hanging outside a car window while driving. *Like a big pregnant, sweaty puppy.* But I could tell by her body language she was working hard to keep her demeanor calm. Her arms were crossed, her muscles tense. She was once again trying to convince me of the great benefit it would bring *her* if I would simply agree to take this drug. Honestly, she may have been right, and if I wasn't pregnant, I may have been more inclined to take it. But all I could think about was how my precious baby girl would be affected by my choices, and so for a third time, I politely said no.

Ironically, this drug was later given to me—with David's consent—as a last-ditch effort to save my life (but more of that story to come).

At this point, I couldn't lie down anymore. In order to catch my breath, I had to sit up and try to rotate my hips as best as I could to get comfortable in the hospital bed, all while the baby was moving and kicking.

The next moment I remember so clearly. It was as though time froze every detail, crisply etched into my memory. In an ICU room, there are huge glass sliding doors, so that for the patient, it's as if you are in a giant fish tank where everyone can see you. I would look out and see the staff constantly talking outside the room or walking by. I looked at the clock hanging on the wall and it appeared to be broken—each second felt like minutes. My focus remained only on breathing. *Just five more minutes.* Just keep breathing for five more minutes; it'll get better, it has to. Then as soon as those five minutes would pass, I would muster up whatever strength I had left and tell myself, *OK I did five minutes, I can do another five minutes.* Just five more minutes. My breathing was extremely labored. Trying not to make any extra movements, I would direct all my energy and focus on breathing and staying alive. As my energy waned, those five-minute segments of focusing on my lungs to contract and expand seemed impossible.

And then I started to feel them…*it's too soon*, I thought. But there was no denying I was feeling them—contractions.

I couldn't talk much at this point because of how much effort it took to just breathe. I saw my OB doctor outside my room talking to ICU doctors and nurses. I picked up my phone and texted her: "I think I might be having contractions." Soon she sent Sherry (the nurse) in and began monitoring the baby even more closely. I was indeed having contractions. Sherry placed the monitors on my belly, walked outside my room and joined the growing group of staff members who were all talking about my care plan.

An overwhelming feeling started to creep in. I was sad that I was all alone in this hospital room starting labor, annoyed that everyone was treating me like I had the plague, and tired that I had to work so hard to breathe. Frankly, I was also frustrated that I couldn't hear or understand what the group of medical personnel were saying as they talked outside my room about me. And also, I was sad that I didn't have the strength to even call David or any of my friends or family. All of those emotions welled up, but I knew I couldn't deal with any of them then, so I tucked them away to deal with later. I had no room for fear or frustration because all my energy and thoughts were on how I was going to keep breathing and get better, nothing else.

So, I just did that.

I would FaceTime David, but not have the strength to hold my phone or say a single word, so I would just sit in silence as he was on the other end of the line. I had so much I wanted to tell him. I wanted to talk to him, to have him beside me. To see the support in his eyes. Instead, I was all alone in this fish tank of a room, with a bunch of medical minds outside my door talking about me, while I was calling the one person I wanted to tell everything to, but physically couldn't utter a word.

This continued for a few hours and I was growing weaker and weaker. This was it. I knew that I no longer had the strength to keep working this hard to breathe. I couldn't sleep, eat or function. A doctor came in and told me they were considering intubating me in the hopes of giving my body a chance to recover quicker. Intubation is done by placing someone in a medical coma, then placing a tube down their throat so that a machine takes over their breathing. This helps their muscles take a break from working so hard. I knew this was a drastic measure but at this point, I was almost relieved. I was exhausted.

As I sat there gasping for air, I saw the ever-growing group outside my room and wondered why they were taking so long to help me. In reality, only a few minutes passed before they walked in. The staff got all the supplies ready and, thankfully, my coworker Jeff was there right beside me, helping with the intubation.

I looked up at him and asked him to pray for me. I don't remember what he said exactly, but I could see so much love and support in his eyes. I was so thankful that I wasn't completely alone during that moment. And then they gave me the medication that put me into a medical coma and proceeded to intubate me. That was the last day I was aware of being pregnant with my daughter.

CHAPTER THREE – QUESTIONS

Whenever I felt alone in my hardship, I already felt defeated.

With all the social distancing, people have become so lonely—both physically and emotionally, causing division in so many aspects of our lives.

If we can be divided, then we have already lost the battle.

Love always wins, even when people don't deserve it. Love always wins.

Asking for help may be a very difficult task, however, it could make all the difference in the outcome of your situation.

Being lonely doesn't necessarily mean you're alone; you could be in a room of people and still feel lonely. For this activity, we will define loneliness as the lack of true companionship and support. Feeling unheard, unseen, or misunderstood. Feeling like you don't belong.

1.) Do you identify with feelings of loneliness? Describe them.

....
....
....
....

2.) Is there anyone you can reach out to? It's important to find the right people who are trustworthy and have your best interests at heart.

....

....

....

....

3.) Is there any hurt you need to forgive? Often, when we are hurt by people, we feel hesitant to trust anyone again. However, healing comes with vulnerability. Isolation never brings healing.

....

....

....

....

4.) What does Jesus say about your relationships? Jesus loves you *so* much, and calls us to live in community.

....

....

....

....

5.) What is one small act of kindness you can do for someone else today? Sometimes, by simply zooming out and not focusing on yourself, it can help get perspective on the situations we are currently faced with.

....

....

....

....

SCRIPTURES

1 John 4:18: "Such love has no fear because perfect love expels all fear. If we are afraid, it is for fear of punishment, and this shows that we have not fully experienced his perfect love."

Colossians 3:13: "Make allowances for each other's faults, and forgive anyone who offends you. Remember, the Lord forgave you, so you must forgive others."

1 John 1:9: "But if we confess our sins to him, he is faithful and just to forgive us our sins and to cleanse us from all wickedness."

FOUR

That's when they started—the nightmares.

People often ask me what it's like to be in a coma. Do you just wake up from a long nap and feel refreshed? Do you hear people talking in the room? Do you see angels? I'm sure each person has a different experience, but in my case, I was on a lot of medication, one of which causes hallucinations. So that's what I got. Crazy-scary hallucinations. Have you ever seen someone on drugs walking down the street and it's as if they are living in a world of their own, having full-blown conversations with their dog? Well, I can now relate.

Every nightmare was my reality. I'm standing in the middle of the ocean floor as hundreds of giant, purple octopuses circle around me. Their tentacles are all facing me. I can hear them swooshing around me, getting closer and closer. But they never quite touch me. They are so big that I can't see anything past them. I can feel my heart pounding in my chest, fear creeping in unchecked. Then, all of a sudden, I'm in a room, I'm tiny, and there are people around me. I want to leave, I need to get back to David and Emily. But I'm stuck; I have some sort of glue on my feet. I try to trick people into letting me go, but all of a sudden, they become giants and I panic, trying to leave. Then, abruptly— I'm riding a big, white horse and we are in a race in a Roman city.

The nightmares continued, one after another, for what felt like a month. Every nightmare had its own story and every story came to a climactic end. Then I would start the next set of dreams. Finally, these nightmares slowly faded—and reality arrived.

CHAPTER FOUR– QUESTIONS

A lie believed as truth will affect your life as though it was true.

Even though I did not experience a lot of fear when I was conscious, the fear of my nightmares was so real that I had to learn how to deal with it.

When we experience strong emotions, they sometimes give us a false label that we grow to believe.

When a fear is shared with a trusted source, it loses its grip of power.

1.) What is your biggest fear?

....

....

....

....

2.) Why are you afraid of that happening?

....

....

....

....

3.) What will happen if your fear comes to pass?

....

....

....

....

4.) What does Jesus say about your fear/outcome/future?

....

....

....

....

When we ask ourselves these questions, the fears begin to unravel and lose their power.

SCRIPTURES

2 Timothy 1:7: "For God has not given us a spirit of fear and timidity, but of power, love and self-discipline."

Philippians 4:6-7: "Don't worry about anything; instead pray about everything. Tell God what you need and thank him for all he has already done. Then you will experience God's peace, which exceeds anything we can understand. His peace will guard your hearts and minds as you live in Christ Jesus."

Psalm 56:3: "But when I am afraid, I will put my trust in you."

1 John 4:18: "Such love has no fear; because perfect love expels all fear. If we are afraid, it is for fear of punishment, and this shows that we have not fully experienced his perfect love."

Isaiah 41:10: "Don't be afraid, for I am with you. Don't be discouraged for I am your God. I will strengthen you and help you. I will hold you up with my victorious right hand."

Psalms 34:4: "I prayed to the Lord and he answered me. He freed me from all my fears."

Proverbs 9:10: "Fear of the Lord is the foundation of wisdom. Knowledge of the Holy One results in good judgment."

FIVE

Besides the octopuses, giants and Roman horse races, I have no memory of what took place from day one to day nine while I was intubated. Therefore, this chapter is written from the recollection and help of my friends and family.

After getting the news that I was intubated, the severity of my sickness hit my family full force. David had called his friends and family and asked everyone to pray for me. Because I was a respiratory therapist, I often shared details about my work and how we intubated our patients with David. He remembered hearing about the severity of the patients that I took care of through the years. He understood the heaviness and the stark reality of what was happening.

DAY ONE
Going from being admitted to the hospital to being intubated is a very big step in the wrong direction. Receiving this news was very emotional for my loved ones. Everyone had a different way of reacting to the news, from "Oh, she's going to be fine" to "Shoot, she's actually really sick". Each person had their own way of dealing but in the beginning, there was a sense of hope and everyone hoped I was going to be OK.

Because I was Covid-positive, they were not allowing any visitors to come in. David often shared with me that one of the hardest things for him was that he was not able to be with me. All day long he would think about me, while torturously knowing that there was nothing he could do for me but pray and believe. That first day not much changed in my condition other than David carefully watching his phone, waiting to hear updates from the doctors. While intubated, the doctors would call to update David once a day about my condition and more frequently if they needed his consent or if there was a big change in my health.

DAY TWO

I was getting even sicker. So sick in fact, that they called David and started to prepare him for the worst. They didn't know how to care for me. And David was starting to get even more worried.

I come from a large community in my church and have many wonderful friends and family (I'm one of ten kids, and David is one of five). Together, that makes a lot of people who were concerned for me. David was the point of contact for communication about my health, so my family and everyone who was worried about me would reach out to him. Naturally, he quickly became overwhelmed as he answered the many questions as quickly as possible.

In addition to the myriad of questions—What is her oxygen saturation? What is her blood count like? What is her ABG showing?—everyone had an opinion to give. "Have you talked to them about…? I read on Google that…" and on and on and on. Suggestions for care varied from essential oils to flying me to Mexico to importing salts from Arabia. There is nothing Google can't cure, right?

David told me that on every phone call with the doctor, he would simply ask, "Is she doing any better?" It was hard to keep up with all the details; all he cared about was me. He just wanted his wife back and everything else was too overwhelming to deal with at the moment. He had to make a lot of difficult medical decisions on my behalf—none of which came with any kind of guarantee to improve my condition.

My family coped quite differently than David. They wanted to know every single little detail about my care, which helped them feel more connected to me and what I was experiencing. But when they would ask David for updates, he didn't have anything to share. This caused even more angst, as information helps us feel in control. Everyone wanted to help, but no one knew how. David reacted as most men might, shelving his emotions and doing the best he could with what little information he had.

My twin sister, Oksana, was friends with a local TV reporter. She met up with her and shared my story on a Portland news channel, asking people to pray. Little did she know that my story would reach national news and eventually even be shared internationally.

That same evening, my family gathered at my parents' house. They prayed and believed that God could—and would— do a miracle. This was the way my family fought battles that were out of our control—gather together, fast, and pray. There were people that we didn't even know who called my family (or shared on social media) about how they were believing and agreeing with us, as a community and the church body, that God would do a miracle.

DAY THREE

I got very sick, and all of my numbers started plummeting. The doctor called David and told him that I may not survive this virus. And even if I did survive, I may need a tracheotomy (a breathing support where they place an artificial airway in your throat that helps you breathe) and that they couldn't guarantee a full recovery for me.

Obviously, this would be heavy news for any husband to hear. The faith that was so strong began to feel a little less brave. Most of the people I talk to say that at this point in my journey, they had to ask the hard question, *What if she doesn't survive? David will be left with two daughters, or even worse, what if the baby doesn't survive either?* The reality of the battle for my life was piercing.

Yet even then, there was a sliver of hope to grasp onto. David, my family, friends, our church, and now most of Clark County were praying and believing that God was going to do a miracle.

DAY FOUR

This was the day I gave birth while in a medical coma. David and I hadn't decided on what we would name our baby, as I mentioned earlier. I had always loved the name Ava, but David was not a huge fan of it. Prior to getting admitted to the hospital, we thought we would have lots of time to decide on her name later. But now that I was intubated, I think he felt he had no choice *but* to name her Ava. Little did I know, the meaning of her name would be so significant. Ava means "breath of life."

The doctors had called David and informed him that my breathing was worsening. They were hoping that by delivering the baby, my lungs would have more room to expand and I would be able to start recovering. They had many conference meetings, all focusing on what would be the best plan to care for me.

They ended up giving me that experimental drug, with David's consent. This was quite literally a last-ditch attempt at saving my life.

Unfortunately, I continued to get sicker.

After continuing to closely monitor me, the hospital staff came to the point of needing to take drastic measures to save my life. Although I was only thirty-three-and-a-half weeks pregnant, my doctor decided that the chances of a healthy birth were high and that by delivering, I could improve my own chances for survival. Unfortunately, giving birth would be placing a lot of stress on my already-weakened body. However, the alternative was waiting and time was not in my favor. So, she gave me the medication to induce labor and they prepared everything to deliver the baby.

I gave birth to Ava in an ICU room, which is very atypical. They were prepared in case I needed an emergency C-section, and they also had everything they needed in the event that Ava was born with complications. Once the medication took effect, my doctors shared that it was as though God Himself was getting everything ready. My body was doing everything it needed to, and when the time came, Ava was born with just a few pushes (apparently, your body can have contractions and push, even when you're completely unconscious). And that's how our little miracle Ava was born, on the first of April, 2020.

When she was born, she was not breathing because all of the medications that were in my body had passed to her through the placenta. She needed to be placed on a ventilator so she that could breathe.

That evening, my baby girl and I were both on ventilators, fighting for our lives.

After I gave birth, it was a huge relief for my family that my lungs finally began improving. Everyone had a second wind of hope and optimism.

David was notified that his daughter was born and stable, and he was able to visit Ava the next day. He was the first and only person who could see Ava due to the Covid rules—they only allowed parents to visit neonates, and even though I was literally unconscious, I still counted as the other parent.

That night—like none other—the church came together and prayed and believed.

A few days after I was home from this whole ordeal, I was talking to my brother Max and, for the first time, I realized that being hospitalized didn't affect just me. My loved ones were also deeply affected. I realized I missed his birthday, so I apologized to him that I wasn't there to celebrate. He replied, "Are you kidding me, Ang—don't be sorry!" I could see tears fill his eyes. I asked him how it was for him while I was intubated. With tears rolling down his cheeks, he responded with, "All I can say is that every night I went to bed with a wet pillow, crying and believing that the Lord would get you through this." It must have been so painful for my family not knowing if I would make it out alive or not.

When David came to see Ava, she was so tiny. She only weighed four and a half pounds. To everyone's surprise, David refused to share pictures of Ava with anyone until I was able to see her for myself. Only after I got to see pictures of Ava did David share them with anyone else. I think it was his way of believing I was going to get better—that I was going to come out of this alive, and that I was going to be able to see our daughter for myself. He refused to believe that he would be a single dad of two girls.

After David went to see and hold Ava, one of the doctors said he could come and see me if he wanted to. This was the first time he was able to see me since dropping me off at the ER a few weeks prior. The doctor escorted David from his daughter who was in the neonatal ICU, to his wife who was in the adult ICU.

He was not allowed to enter my room; he was only able to stand outside the door and look at me through the glass.

What he saw was me hooked up to all my IVs, the breathing machine and the myriad of tubes and lines that were attached to me. He said it was so crazy to see me breathing so fast. It looked unnatural. He was allowed to stay outside my room for a few minutes and was then escorted back out.

With his wife and daughter so sick, David experienced many emotions and stress, but he kept busy to keep his feelings at bay. He would work all day, come home, shower, and then go to my parents' house and be with our older daughter so that he wouldn't have to deal with the reality of what was happening.

DAY FIVE

Because delivering a baby (even under normal conditions), places stress on a woman's body, when they delivered Ava, I got worse. So much worse, in fact, that they didn't know what else to do or even try. They considered transferring me to another hospital but were unsure if I would survive being moved. They also knew that if they needed different interventions, they could get help from a local, bigger hospital much more quickly—so they decided to keep me put.

I was getting one hundred percent oxygen support with a very high level of positive end-expiratory pressure (PEEP). PEEP was another way to help oxygenate my body with a ventilator. At the hospital, we like to keep PEEP levels as low as possible; five is a level when we consider extubating (taking the breathing tube out and bringing the patient back out of coma). For reference, my PEEP levels were between 22 and 26. Even with all the support my lungs were getting, they were still having a very difficult time effectively oxygenating the rest of my body. In addition to Covid,

I was now developing pneumonia and my troponin levels were increasing, showing that I was sustaining some heart damage.

During the night, it would get even worse. Every hour I was alive was a victory. I talked to one of my nurses afterward and she said, "Honestly, most of us were not sure that you were going to survive."

My dad was so stressed that he would spend hours just mowing the yard and praying. My mom kept busy by watching my older daughter Emmie, believing and praying. My sisters would chat in group texts and cope any way they knew how. My friends gathered and prayed for me. Some cried, some got angry, some were in denial. No one had any guarantee I would survive.

Living through a situation so hopeless caused a dependency on God like never before. They all had to press in and hear His still, small voice. This was exactly the time Jesus had to step in. People who hadn't prayed in years, prayed for me. People who didn't even believe in God, prayed. And all of those prayers were not in vain.

DAYS SIX and SEVEN
The days proceeded in a similar fashion. I would get slightly better, then slightly worse. They tried multiple times to wean me off the ventilator but I would fail all of the tests and continue to decline.

Every day, my family would grow more and more concerned. One of my brothers even said, "We didn't know if we should prepare for a miracle or a funeral."

Hundreds of people were believing and praying for a miracle, believing that our God could do the impossible. Everyone prayed for the staff, for God to use them in this miracle, for them to know what to do, to have wisdom and—when all else failed—that God would have the final word.

David stayed busy during the day, but when evening came, he was alone. He was left to fight the fear and worry on his own; he would weep before the Lord to spare my life.

DAY EIGHT

They called David and told him they were considering a tracheotomy for me. At this point, the prolonged effects of low oxygenation may have left permanent damage and they warned him to prepare for the worst.

When this news came to my family, they refused to believe it. They prayed and believed that even when doctors can't predict the outcome, our God has the final say. The entire community believed God could do a miracle—and He did.

DAY NINE

David got a phone call telling him I was breathing on my own and doing quite well. This, after the preceding day's news that brought fear over possible long-term damage. "How is that possible?" he asked. "Just yesterday you weren't sure she would *survive*—and today she's extubated?"

There was a time when everyone lost hope, but against all hope, I miraculously got better. I believe with all my heart that God partners with the hands of medical professionals and I am forever grateful to each person who cared for me. I also believe in prayer and that God Himself has the final say.

My family rejoiced that I was finally extubated. My dad would often say, "This was truly an Easter miracle, because God resurrected Angela." They didn't talk to me until that evening, but when they finally FaceTimed me, they could tell I was obviously still on a lot of medication. I would have moments of clarity, but then I would say crazy things and tell them to get a helicopter and get me out of the hospital because people were "trying to kill me". I was going through what is called ICU delirium. I didn't have a moment where I was "back". There were times when I felt like I was so close to having a moment of clarity, but then I'd go right back to crazy-nightmare land. This continued for so long that it took me a while to grasp what was actual reality and not make-belief. This back and forth of almost-reality, then night terrors continued on and on. I was still hallucinating for a while until all of the medications that were in my system wore off. During this time, I was very confused about where I was and what was going on. I kept asking where my baby was. I have no clue how many times people must have told me the same thing over and over. But the day finally came—I was out of the delirium and woke up.

CHAPTER FIVE – QUESTIONS

After coming out of the coma, a lot of attention was given to me, making sure I was OK and getting help. But very few people reached out to David or my family and asked them how they were doing. Considering my story ended with such a good outcome, it almost felt like they shouldn't have any other emotion *but* happiness.

I believe there's such a thing as second-hand trauma. Where the trauma of someone we love has such a deep effect on us, it traumatizes us also. The first step toward healing is validating second-hand trauma. Your emotions are valid.

Although it was not you who went through the trauma, it still has an effect on you. And that second-hand trauma needs to be dealt with also. It can feel just as real as going through it yourself. Maybe you saw a sibling get yelled at, molested, or hit, and it forever scarred you. Or maybe someone you love got bullied and you now get triggered whenever people tease each other, even if it's playful? Common second-hand trauma is also experienced through divorce or relational betrayal.

1.) Have you experienced second-hand trauma?

....

....

....

....

2.) What has that situation caused you to believe about yourself, other people and/or God? (E.g., no one will ever be close to me because _____, I can't allow anyone to see this part of my life, God abandoned me when I needed Him most, etc.)

....

....

....

....

3.) What does God want you to believe about that negative belief instead?

....

....

....

....

4.) It's not uncommon for healing to take time and for occasional emotions to resurface after a traumatic event. Healing is simply going in the right direction. Instant results are often what we strive for, but similar to physical healing, emotional healing can take time. Learn to celebrate every little victory.

....

....

....

....

SCRIPTURES

Romans 8:18: "Yet what we suffer now is nothing compared to the glory he will reveal to us later."

1 Peter 5:10: "In his kindness, God called you to share in his eternal glory by means of Christ Jesus. So after you have suffered a little while, he will restore, support, and strengthen you and he will place you on a firm foundation."

Psalms 147:3: "He heals the broken-hearted and bandages their wounds."

Job 36:15: "But by means of their suffering, he rescues those who suffer. For he gets their attention through adversity."

Psalms 34:18: "The Lord is close to the broken-hearted; He rescues those whose spirits are crushed."

Psalms 51:17: "The sacrifice you desire is a broken spirit; you will not reject a broken and repentant heart, O God."

SIX

As I opened my eyes, I felt so hazy, not really knowing if I was still in a dream or if I was finally back to reality. I watched employees walk past my room. I could hear distant noises but felt very drowsy and would fall right back asleep.

Finally, the moment came when I was a little more lucid and as I looked around me, I saw pictures hung on the walls of my ICU room. Pictures of my husband, my older daughter, Emily, my family and friends, and a sign that said, "Healthy baby girl, Ava." I must have looked at those words for hours until it dawned on me that that was probably my daughter's name. I looked down and saw that I no longer had a baby in my belly. *How on earth did I give birth while in a coma?* I didn't remember a single moment. I still had so much medication in my system that I felt nothing. I didn't have the energy to be happy or sad—or to really feel anything at all. But my gaze wandered back to the wall again: healthy baby Ava. Ava.

David must have named her 'Ava', I thought to myself.

I later found out that David picked her middle name all on his own: Ava Angela.

Still confused and a bit hazy, a nurse came in to help me pump my breast milk. Apparently, they had been pumping for me while I was intubated. When I found that out I felt a bit exposed, but on the other hand, I had been planning to breastfeed and certainly couldn't have done it myself. Then the nurse broke the news to me that my breast milk was worthless. "You were on a medication that can pass through your breast milk, so we have to give your baby donor milk for now. You can still pump; however, we will have to throw away your milk for fourteen days," she said.

Confused, I asked, "What medication? You ended up giving me that experimental drug?"

"Yes, there was a time when you were in a coma and we really didn't know if you would make it. This medication was the last straw for you." For some reason, it was borderline comical for me to hear that news. I instantly imagined how happy that drug rep lady must have been. I guess there's a reason you have a guardian who makes choices on your behalf. I knew for a fact David would never do something without doing his research so I wasn't concerned about it. And so, I began the exhausting journey of "pumping and dumping". All that liquid gold was being poured down the drain.

When I woke up from the coma, I had lost forty pounds from my initial admittance weight. The baby only weighed four and a half pounds at birth, so a good deal of the weight loss was me losing muscle. When someone is paralyzed, they lose a lot of muscle tone from not using their most basic muscles for everyday movements. The term "if you don't use it, you lose it" is very applicable when someone is intubated. My arms and legs had an awkward, stick-like appearance. I felt weak just moving my arm—I had virtually no strength. My arms would shake just trying to sit myself up in bed. I didn't have the strength to even adjust a pillow.

I also discovered a feeding tube in my nose that went to my stomach, as I couldn't eat solid food yet. I hated that tube so much; anytime I would move, the tube would yank on my nostrils and it felt as though it was pulling on my nerves. I was ready to get it out. In addition, I had a huge IV in my neck called a central line that is used to get medication directly to the heart, which then helps get the medication dispersed throughout the body quicker. I also had three or four IVs in my hands, a blood pressure cuff around my arm that went off every fifteen to thirty minutes, and a beautiful green hospital gown that matched my eye color (at least!) My hair hadn't been washed or brushed for who knows how long, I had no makeup on and a sweaty aroma about me. I mean, I was *quite* the beauty queen.

So basically, we were back to where we started. Any time I needed help with anything, the nurses would fully gown up to help me. I felt bad, but genuinely could not do much on my own.

The next day, I finally felt like I could call my family. The staff gave me my phone; the time was finally here! The moment I could FaceTime David and actually speak. For the first time, I felt happy. But as I took my phone, my fingers failed to do what they'd done thousands of times before. I was trying to type, but it felt similar to the way it feels after you have been out in the snow and try to text. My happiness quickly turned to annoyance as my fingers just wouldn't cooperate. Determined, it took me thirty minutes until I was able to type the letters *d* and *a* in my contacts and see David's name pop up.

I clicked the FaceTime button and the phone rang. "Hi, baby," he said. I could finally see his face! Wow, he had never looked more handsome.

Tears began to well up in my eyes and trickle down my cheeks. My voice, ever so raspy from having the breathing tube in my throat, managed to croak out, "Hey love. How are you?"

"Oh, hey baby, how are you feeling today, better than yesterday?"

Yesterday? I thought. "What do you mean?" I asked.

"You don't remember calling me yesterday? You have been calling us, ranting about how everyone is trying to kill you. You wanted us to helicopter you to another hospital," he laughed. "Are you better today?"

What have I done? I thought to myself. I was so mortified. *Who else have I called?* Overwhelming shame, mixed with confusion, filled me. I didn't even know who to be angry with. I was just so embarrassed. "Yeah babe, you were yelling at the staff. Throwing stuff. But you're OK now. How are you?" David continued. His words pierced my heart. *What had I done?* I thought. We talked for a few more minutes, but all I could think about was what all these people were going to think about me. I just wanted to hide from embarrassment.

At this point, the speech therapist came in so I had to say goodbye to David. I threw aside the shame and embarrassment, quickly placing them on my growing "to deal with later" shelf. I bravely put on a smile for the therapist. We were going to do a test to see if I could finally get this nasty feeding tube out. I was given ice to see if I could swallow the melting water. *No problem*, I thought, *let's do this!* However, my bravado quickly faded because as soon as I tried to swallow that ice water, I went into a crazy cough.

"I'm so sorry," she told me. "We are just going to have to wait a little longer." I was annoyed, but sadly agreed with her; I was still trying to catch my breath after my coughing spree. I understood the feeding tube was not ready to come out yet. My airway muscles were so weak that if I tried to eat food or even have ice water I would end up with food or water in my lungs, and not my stomach. So, we had to wait until my muscles were strong enough to handle guiding things into my stomach.

Shortly after, a physical therapist came in. He seemed nice

and I couldn't wait to get out of bed. I hadn't even tried to get up, but I was determined not to have to use the bedpan anymore. Anyone who has ever been hospitalized knows the feeling of being confined to a bed and, to top it off, having to use a bedpan. I knew the physical therapist had a big say in when I could do stuff on my own, so I was ready to go.

Still bleeding after giving birth, I got help to put on that cute, mesh granny underwear with a pad, and pulled my gown around me. I was ready to walk! But just pushing myself up from the lying position, my arm gave way and I fell back onto my pillow. "My arms are just being weird," I said with a hesitant smile. "It's OK, let me try again." I pushed with all my strength and although shakily, those little twigs of mine pushed me up to a sitting position. I was so proud of myself! *Now just swing your legs over the bed*, I told myself. Unfortunately, even with mustering all of my strength, I couldn't get my legs to the side of the bed on my own. My abs were floating somewhere in my postpartum belly and my back and legs refused to work together. The therapist came and gently helped get my legs over the side of the bed while a nurse gently guided my back. Almost immediately, I broke out into a sweat. My heart was pounding and I thought I was going to faint.

Gently, the physical therapist helped me back into a lying position. *What is going on?* I thought.

"It's OK," he said. "We can try again tomorrow."

With a smile, I lay back on the bed, trying to hide the pain and soreness coursing through my whole body. Muscles I didn't even know I had were sore. I secretly hoped he didn't see how truly difficult it was for me. My job was to trick him into letting me try again tomorrow. When it came to physical therapy, I felt I needed to be strong and prove I was capable. I was going to go back to sitting up and walking around in no time. I craved to go back to "normal".

As soon as he left, I sank into the mattress, with every muscle of my body groaning. Who knew you used that many muscles just to sit up in bed? Soon after, the nurse came in and gave me shots to control the nausea, pain and my daily blood thinner medication.

My therapy continued. Next, it was the occupational therapist's turn. She began by asking me about my progress with trying to relearn daily activities. The truth was that I had to really focus and use all my strength to do simple things like pulling the sheets over myself, texting, or brushing my teeth. Today, she had come to help me brush my hair. She asked if I wanted to try. I was so tired, yet too stubborn to admit that I needed help. That's when I noticed my hair was braided. "Who braided my hair?" I asked.

"Oh—Kara, Pam, Dawn, Julia, and some more of your coworkers came in and braided your hair while you were in a coma. They also hung all these pictures in your room, as well as in Ava's room in the neonatal ICU." Wow, I hadn't even thought about the fact that someone had put these pictures up…

The occupational therapist gave me the hairbrush and I started to brush my hair. I was about three strokes in and my hands were shaking. Sweat began accumulating on my forehead and my breathing was getting labored. It soon became so hard that I physically could not hold up my arms. The occupational therapist noticed that I was struggling. Maybe it was the not-so-subtle arm-shaking, or maybe the beads of sweat popping up on my upper lip, but she put her hand on my arm, took the brush and began to do it herself. With gloves on and her full PPE get-up including a helmet and gown, she touched my hand…and I felt so much love at that moment.

"Thank you," I said.

It was the first time in a long time that someone took the time to just touch my hand. I didn't realize that I hadn't had any affectionate touch in so long. All the staff had been amazing—so professional and caring—but her actions clearly displayed that she wasn't in a rush. She just held my hand. Little did I know all the other acts of love, care, and kindness that so many other staff members did for me while I was intubated: the staff members who came in to just sit beside me, my OB who massaged my legs, the nurses who cared for me like they would for a family member, the doctors who met tirelessly to find the best approach to my care. Taking all this in, I simply sat there in the ICU bed with her brushing my hair, still catching my breath from the few brush strokes I had attempted.

The following day, I called David as well as a few friends. It made the day feel like it passed by a little faster. I wanted to text back people who were writing to me, but my fingers were still working in slow motion and my brain still felt very foggy. Every task seemed to take more effort to accomplish. The day brought the same round of visitors to my room. First, the speech therapist came in. This time, however, I was prepared. I focused so hard on swallowing that ice water. And I did it! Hallelujah! I hated that feeding tube and was ready for it to come out.

"Not so fast," she said, "we still need to get jello and applesauce down." The thought of jello sounded quite literally amazing at that moment. Thankfully, I was able to keep it down. It didn't go down easy and I coughed and choked a lot, but we did it. I hadn't graduated to applesauce yet. But hey, we made it to jello!

It was a good day so far, but my acting was about to be put to the test when the physical therapist walked in. I was ready to go. He came in, and I knew I was going to make it today. Just like before, I mustered up all my energy and sat up. "How are you feeling?" he asked.

"Good," I lied. My heart was pounding and I was feeling

very light-headed. He slowly walked to the other side of the room and got a walker, which was perfect because it gave me just enough time to regain my composure and for the dizziness to subside. He brought the walker over to me, put those red anti-slip socks on my feet, and I was doing it! I placed my hand around that gray handle, my heart pounding, sweat dripping down my face, and with all that I had in me, I placed my feet on the ground and stood up. My legs and arms were shaking violently. It must have looked like I was trying to dance the chicken dance. Exactly four seconds later, I sat back down on the bed.

"Yay! How was that?" he asked.

"Not too bad," I said, faking a smile.

"OK, let's do it again," he said.

"Yes… yeah, that's a great idea," I said hesitantly, and so we tried again. But this time, I was able to stand for fifteen seconds. And bit by bit throughout the day, I was able to go from standing, to pivoting, to sitting in a chair.

Although one might think that the chair wouldn't be that different from lying in bed, it exhausted me—I think maybe because you use more muscles while having to hold yourself up. I could only sit in the chair for ten to fifteen minutes before I began to feel weak and light-headed and my whole body was aching again. I knew I couldn't sit in the chair for much longer, yet I also felt so bad because I constantly needed so much help from everyone. Simply getting in and out of bed meant the nurse would have to gown up and put on all the PPE just to enter my room. Feeling guilty that I was making their job harder, I took that emotion and added it to my very large, ever-growing shelf of emotions I would deal with later.

Finally, I couldn't take it any longer and called the nurse in to help me back into bed. I was exhausted from a very hard day of standing and pivoting. Then, just when I had finally caught my breath, another nurse came in to help me pump. Pump, and then dump.

Nighttime was always the hardest. I couldn't find a good rhythm and constantly felt as though I was in a dark fishbowl. Nurses did not come in as often and not as many staff members were around. I remembered that back when I was working in the ICU, some patients would ask to keep the curtains open. I had found it odd then, but now I understood. Being in the ICU day and night, all alone with only staff to keep you company ramps up the feelings of loneliness. Some of the challenges that arose at night were because there were no activities to distract me, no people to call or extra staff members coming in. The muscle aches felt more painful and the nausea from the feeding tube was more extreme. My brain was racing and my body was exhausted. All the day's activities seemed to be whooshing around in my brain, yet I didn't know how to process them, or even what to think. I would just wait for morning to come and hope to fall asleep somewhere in between all that was going on inside. Finally, the morning did come.

Every so often, a coworker would walk by and wave at me. I loved feeling less lonely that way. Then my coworkers Julia and Melissa came in, all gowned-up—I couldn't have been happier to see them. They were fellow respiratory therapists and were working that day, so they popped in on their break. "How are you, ladies?" I asked.

"Good," they said. "We came to paint your nails and shave your legs. That husband of yours can't have you coming home with those unpainted nails!"

I laughed; I couldn't believe it! Sure enough, they talked with me, massaged my feet, shaved my legs and painted my nails. They gave me so much more than a pedicure: they filled me with strength and love through their kindness. I was so grateful.

CHAPTER SIX – QUESTIONS

When I was going through all my hardships—while I had many people love and support me—during the hardest times, I honestly didn't know how to cope. So I just did what most of us do: I shelved all my emotions. I had a season of just surviving. It wasn't until I was doing my evening routine one night—crying quietly in bed, so as not to wake David—that I got a sudden thought. *It would have been easier if I hadn't survived.* It was at that moment that I had to make a choice: was I going to agree with this emotion, or was I going to turn to God?

Sometimes we think that if we don't deal with an emotion, it'll eventually die. However, as much as we would love for that to be true, the reality is that an emotion placed on a shelf is still alive; the only way emotions are truly dealt with is when we bring them out to light and show the reality of what is going on.

That was the day I chose to partner with being OK to start the messy journey to emotional health. I was the one who started to reach out to my community, I was the one who called for help. I took tiny steps to get my breakthrough. In the beginning, I didn't even know how to let anyone into the hurt I was carrying. But day by day, I chose to let people in, to seek help, and to see my situation from God's perspective.

When we don't deal with emotions, we start to camp out and live in the place of hurt. *Poor me and my hardships, and all I have gone through.* But our emotions are meant to bring us closer to God and people; they are meant to help bring healing to a place that's hurting. Let's break out of that camp and move into a place of healing!

There have been times in my marriage when David hurt me and I wanted to forgive him quickly, but I felt that if I forgave him *too* quickly, he would think it was OK to hurt me again. So as a way to protect my emotions, I would stay mad longer than I actually was, to prove a point—that he'd really hurt me, and that I hoped he wouldn't hurt me again.

Unfortunately, I was putting my emotions above our relationship. The ability to forgive quickly is a wonderful way to build relationships and to have better emotional health.

Forgiving does not mean your hurt was not deep, it means your love is deeper. And healing can happen even to the most real and deepest of hurts.

1.) Do you have a hurt from yesterday (or further back) that you are still holding on to?

....

....

....

....

2.) If so, why are you still holding on to it?

....

....

....

....

3.) What benefit has holding on to hurt brought into your life? What negative outcomes have come from holding on to unforgiveness?

....

....

....

....

4.) What does Jesus say about your hurt? What does Jesus say about the person who hurt you?

....

....

....

....

SCRIPTURES

Ephesians 4:32: "Instead, be kind to one another, tender hearted, forgiving one another, just as God, through Christ has forgiven you."

Mark 11:25: "But when you are praying, first forgive anyone you are holding a grudge against, so that your Father in heaven will forgive your sins, too."

James 5:16: "Confess your sins to each other and pray for each other so that you may be healed. The earnest prayer of a righteous person has great power and produces wonderful results."

Ephesians 1:7: "He is so rich in kindness and grace that he purchased our freedom with the blood of his son and forgave our sins."

James 5:14: "Are any of you sick? You should call for the elders of the church to come and pray over you, anointing you with oil in the name of the Lord. Such prayer offered in faith will heal the sick, and the Lord will make you well. And if you have committed any sins, you will be forgiven."

SEVEN

My days were so booked with appointments that I nearly forgot about Ava. She was born while I was still unconscious and intubated, so not only did I not remember a single detail of her birth, I also hadn't had any face-to-face connection with her yet. I hadn't really thought about the logistics of it—*how was she actually born?* I knew that she was in the neonatal intensive care unit and that while she was doing well, she still only weighed four and a half pounds and had a feeding tube (just like her momma) because she couldn't eat on her own. I realized I was so busy with all the things I needed for my recovery that I hadn't even fully grasped the fact that I had another daughter. A strong wave of guilt filled me. *How could I not think about her every moment?* I knew I loved her, but I hadn't even met her or seen her yet. It's like my mind knew I had a child, but my heart and emotions hadn't caught up to that reality yet.

The nurses, being as amazing as they were, found a way for me to FaceTime Ava. My heart raced as excitement filled me. At this point, I could pull myself up fairly easily and adrenaline flooded me. I was finally going to see my little girl! They handed me the iPad, the phone rang and a NICU nurse answered. For the first time, I was able to see my sweet, tiny girl. She was so small and perfect. So sweet and so blurry (because, of course, the iPad kept glitching). But I got to see her and she was mine. Tears rolled down my cheeks; the emotions all flooded in. Joy, happiness, love, along with a huge wave of heaviness came over me as I was flooded with guilt. I could almost feel the weight plop down on my chest. She was all alone, so tiny and with no one to hold her or hug her. David was the only one who was allowed to see her, but he worked all day and was only able to come in the evenings.

I knew she was well taken care of by the staff—but knowing that she was in a room only a few stories above me, yet I couldn't hug, kiss or even clearly see her, pierced me. I didn't know what to do with my emotions. I didn't know how to feel, and so I remained focused on trying to see her little face and talk to her as much as I could. We had a short conversation but then the nurse had to go to another patient, so I said goodbye and hung up. It was so sweet to see her and before I could even process everything that happened, my alarm rang and it was time to pump and dump again. I swiped at the tears that were building up, shoved all my emotions away and continued on.

Soon, the speech therapist came in. Today, I would graduate to applesauce and there was no way she would stop me. I tried at least five times and finally did it! She was hesitant, but after my intense cajoling, she let me have applesauce and jello. I was living my best life! The next goal I set for myself was to get that feeding tube out. Then it was on to the physical therapist. I worked harder than ever and took my first steps. I couldn't talk or look or even think about anything other than moving. My feelings, all my attention, all my focus, all my strength was in taking a single step.

But I did it.

I took a few steps and sat in the chair.

"How was that?" he asked.

I responded, with a real smile this time, "It was good." "Good" might have been an overstatement at that point, but I did it! *I will continue to fake it till I make it,* I thought. That day was momentous for me as I also graduated to being able to use a commode next to my bed. I could finally go to the restroom on my own!

Chapter Seven – Questions

Having two kids less than a year apart put so much on my plate. I was so busy caring for everyone, I couldn't—and didn't—take care of myself. The postpartum and newborn phase of parenting is exceptionally hard with the lack of sleep, time and energy. But during that time, I had an evening when I wanted to spend time in prayer and I clearly heard God tell me, "Angela, I just want you to rest. I'll be here when you wake up." It was such a beautiful, fatherly love. He saw my burnout and exhaustion.

God is on our side, He is fighting for us. I started to be extremely intentional with my time and energy.

Having very little alone time, I started to play worship music while feeding the girls or listening to a podcast while changing diapers. I listened to an audio book while driving and during the girls' naps, I would just talk to God as I enjoyed my now-cold cup of tea. The biggest change was that I would be aware of God—aware that He was always with me, that I had a helper by my side, that He had not left me in my exhaustion but was right beside me.

God gives us permission to take care of ourselves. God created you to be the healthiest and best version of yourself. When we care too much for all those around us and neglect to tap into the helping hand of God, we are robbing our loved ones (and ourselves) of seeing the best version of us.

1.) What are small ways you can include God in your

everyday activities?

....

....

....

....

2.) What does a healthy person look like?

....

....

....

....

3.) What is one small, realistic goal you can make to achieve a healthier version of yourself?

....

....

....

....

SCRIPTURES

Ecclesiastes 3:1: "For everything there is a season, a time for every activity under heaven."

Psalm 46:10: "Be still, and know that I am God! I will be honored by every nation. I will be honored throughout the world."

Lamentation 3:26: "So it is good to wait quietly for salvation from the Lord."

Ecclesiastes 5:3a: "Too much activity gives you restless dreams."

Psalm 136:23: "He remembers us in our weakness. His faithful love endures forever."

Proverbs 16:3: "Commit your actions to the Lord and your plans will succeed."

2 Corinthians 12:9: "And each time he said, 'My grace is all you need. My power works best in weakness.' So now I am glad to boast about my weaknesses, so that the power of Christ can work through me."

Ephesians 3:20: "Now to God, who is able, through his mighty power at work within us, to accomplish infinitely more than we might ask or imagine."

Isaiah 40:31: "But those who trust in the Lord will find new strength. They will soar high on wings like eagles. They will run and not grow weary. They will walk and not faint."

EIGHT

Evening came and I got to talk to David more. The phone calls were challenging because we would talk for a little while and then he would need to work. Then he would call me back, but I would be busy with pumping or trying to eat applesauce or peeing. And though loneliness crept in again, every now and then someone I knew would walk by and wave, and that made it bearable.

The next day came and it was almost as though the sun came out. I was so done with the smell of the feeding tube, I was ready to get it out by signing an against medical advice (AMA) form, where you can opt out of medical treatment recommendations as a patient, taking all liability upon yourself. Thankfully, the speech therapist came and after my skillful persuasion, she agreed that I was indeed ready and removed it. Although the feeding tube was out, the smell was still there. It was as though someone had smeared rotten tomatoes along the inside of my nose. The applesauce and jello somehow got harder to eat. I kept choking on them, but the idea of reinserting that feeding tube kept me quite motivated to eat as carefully as I could to avoid choking. The stomach pain was getting sharper, and the nausea more severe as my stomach had to relearn what to do with food. I threw up often and they gave me more nausea medication.

My motor skills were drastically improving with occupational therapy. I was able to brush my teeth, even though occasionally my hand would slip and my cheek got a minty brush. Texting was getting much better; I estimate I was at about thirty percent of my former texting speed. That day I walked two whole laps around my small ICU room, pushing myself so hard that I had to take a midday nap. They came in and took out a large central IV line that was in my neck, where I now have a scar as a friendly reminder of my ICU stay.

I was able to FaceTime my family and friends; we talked for a while and my siblings started to amusingly recall my moments of delirium. *How embarrassing to be so crazy!* "Guys, we shouldn't have told her," my brother Dan said. And everyone started laughing. I smiled very awkwardly and faked that someone walked into my room, hanging up just so that I didn't have to deal with the topic. Growing up in a Slavic community, I was raised to have a very proper image. And delirium did not fit into that ideal at all. I was humiliated that I had been talking crazy but didn't know how to deal with the shame of the things I'd done while delirious.

Nights continued to be hard. Insomnia was real and I didn't know what to do with myself. And that night specifically—nausea kicked in hard. I started throwing up over and over and felt weaker and weaker. My stomach felt like a needle was pricking me. I guess this is what happens when you get weaned off a feeding tube and introduced to applesauce and jello. But with the help of nurses and medication, I finally got more comfortable and was able to fall asleep.

CHAPTER EIGHT – QUESTIONS

As I mentioned, I was mortified at how I had behaved while under medication. Although that moment in my life was outside of my control, there have been other incidents where I contributed to embarrassing myself.

There are times when we feel ashamed of how we act, for saying something embarrassing in a crowd or disappointing someone.

Most of the time, we are harder on ourselves than we are on others.

1.) What is one embarrassing moment you have a hard time letting go of?

....
....
....
....

2.) How did that moment make you feel? What did you believe about yourself?

....
....
....
....

3.) How does Jesus see you in that moment?

....

....

....

....

4.) Do you need to forgive someone (or yourself), for doing that?

....

....

....

....

SCRIPTURES

Psalm 25:7: "Do not remember the rebellious sins of my youth. Remember me in light of your unfailing love, for you are merciful, O Lord."

Romans 5:5: "And this hope will not lead to disappointment. For we know how dearly God loves us, because he has given the Holy Spirit to fill out hearts with his love."

Psalm 42:11: "Why am I discouraged? Why is my heart so sad? I will put my hope in God! I will praise him again, my Savior and my God."

Proverbs 12:25: "Worry weighs a person down; an encouraging word cheers a person up."

NINE

The big day finally came—I was graduating from the intensive care unit to a general care unit! This was a huge step that didn't just move me up one floor, it moved me closer to going home.

I had another physical therapy appointment that day and I worked hard. The therapist said that I was finally strong enough to walk, but that I needed to make sure to walk with someone's assistance since I was not yet strong enough to walk on my own. I was thrilled. And so they began the process of preparing to transfer me to the general care unit in the hospital. They put a mask on me, covered me with a sheet, and as the door opened and they wheeled me out, to my surprise, a row of staff members had lined up clapping for me. It felt so good that they were there celebrating this milestone in my recovery. What I didn't realize was how hard each one of them fought for my recovery. Each staff member that clapped for me had spent hours and days caring and believing that I was going to get better. And so, we all celebrated my graduation out of the ICU.

My new room was much bigger and had a large window facing the parking garage. As they rolled me in, the nurse helped me to the bed and got me settled. I asked if I could shower and to my surprise, she said yes. She said someone would come in to help. "I think the physical therapist said I could be on my own if I'm strong enough," I lied. I one hundred percent lied. I just wanted to shower in peace without a stranger with me while I'm butt naked.

I walked into the shower using the walker. Covered with the IVs that were still attached to my hands, I covered them with a waterproof patch and slowly removed my gown. For the first time, I got a full-length view of myself in the mirror. My postpartum belly was all flabby, my arms and legs had that awkward, skinny look—none of that "Oh she's cute" kind-of-skinny. More like "How are those chicken legs holding her up?" kind-of-skinny. My arms were bruised from what must have been countless needle pokes, my face oddly bony, missing muscle tone. I stood there for maybe all of five seconds, but then suddenly felt weak, so I sat down on the stool in the shower. I proceeded to turn on the water and felt the most refreshing warm water touch my face. Perfection couldn't have described that moment any better. The water felt so good! I hadn't showered in almost three weeks and this was beyond glorious. I put the shampoo in my hair and started to massage my head, but my arm didn't have the strength to keep going so I would stop for a few minutes, gather more strength and try again. Hoping most of the shampoo was rinsed out, I was starting to regret not getting help with the shower and sat for a bit longer. Then I started to feel light-headed. I turned off the water and sat for what felt like a long while, to the point that the warm water droplets were now cold on my skin. I didn't have the strength to even dry myself off, so completely soaked, I proceeded to put on my clothes. My arms were shaking and my legs were quivering. Shockingly, I made it back to the bed. My hair was still soaked and all knotted, but brushing it would have to be a task for later because I didn't have an ounce of strength left in me. Up on this floor, the nurses rarely came into the room, other than to give me pain medication, a shot in my stomach to thin my blood, or to take my vitals. Otherwise, I was left all alone.

I so badly wanted to talk with someone, but holding the phone up during a conversation required more energy than I had. So, I sat in silence. It felt good to just sit for a little while. Shortly after, a few of my coworkers came to visit. It was the most refreshing and, at the same time, the most draining experience. It was like my emotional health wanted to have them nearby, but my physical body was just too exhausted. I didn't know if I could tell them that I was too tired to talk, that I just simply wanted someone with me. I didn't want to have to talk or answer questions, I just didn't want to be left alone. However, their company did serve as a good distraction from the exhaustion creeping into every corner of my mind. The moment they left the room I again felt so, so tired. It was as if I had just gone through the hardest workout of my life. I sat there trying to regain my strength as my alarm went off to pump and dump.

The doctor came in and said he didn't know when he would let me go home. "You're kind of like the guinea pig, we haven't had many Covid cases and we're still trying to figure out the best way to treat you. I had a patient who we kept until she was getting consistent negative Covid testing—which in her case, took thirty days," he explained.

Thirty days kept echoing over and over in my mind. Then I asked him when I could see Ava. He responded by telling me that once I could get two negative Covid tests in a row, I would be able to see her. *Wow*, I thought, *it could be another thirty days before I even get to see my little girl*. A huge wave of sadness engulfed me. My heart sank...so this was going to be home for the next several weeks, and seeing my daughter in person might not happen for another month. Disappointment filled me, but I proceeded to brush it off. I needed to save every ounce of my energy. My next step was to call David and explain everything to him.

I then FaceTimed with my older daughter Emmie, but ended up feeling even more guilty. My mom was watching her, my other daughter was in the NICU, my husband was all alone—I felt like I was failing. Failing as a mom and failing as a wife. I knew these emotions were more than I could handle and I was not ready to fight that battle yet, so as usual, I tucked them onto that shelf of emotions to deal with later (mind you, at this point it was getting quite full).

Thankfully, my OB came in. I could tell she wasn't in a rush; she had come just to talk to me. I was glad to finally be able to ask some questions. I started with, "So what happened to me while I was intubated?" Our hour-long conversation helped me fill in some of the gaps of what had happened from when I was intubated to when I woke up.

She told me that once I started getting sicker, they knew it was time to intubate me. My breathing was becoming too labored and I was getting quite weak. They contacted David and told him I was getting worse. After I was intubated, they continued to monitor me carefully, and though I got better for a little while, I then began to get much worse. My lungs were constantly struggling and they became more concerned for the health of both me and my baby. Unfortunately, I continued getting worse day after day. They had many meetings with ICU, OB and NICU doctors because my case was so unique. Drugs that might help me might also be quite harmful to the baby, and vice versa. They discussed my best care plan for hours and hours. They gave me every medication they thought was best for my recovery. All medications for treating Covid at that point were experimental, and she explained that they had no other choice but to give me that experimental drug. Their sole focus was my survival and my baby's survival. So that's when they decided I was going to give birth to my baby while I was still intubated and in a coma.

From a medical point of view, this was a very complicated procedure because they needed to have every detail addressed and protocols in place in case the birth had complications. My OB was prepared to do an emergency C-section in the ICU while having two sets of all her personal protective gear on. They didn't want to expose the baby to Covid, nor complicate my health.

To spare you all the details, it was a very complex process that included many staff members working seamlessly together. They prepared a room next door to mine to take Ava into as soon as she was born. Due to all the medication they had been giving me, Ava was not able to breathe on her own right away. The medications did affect her; her muscles were too relaxed for her to breathe, so they ended up intubating her for a day. So, both Ava and I were intubated simultaneously. This fact—to this day—still makes me tear up.

My OB went on to explain that after I delivered Ava, I proceeded to get worse. So bad in fact, that many thought I would not make it. David later told me they were preparing him for the worst-case scenario: that I may die. And even if I did somehow survive, they said that I might need to have a tracheotomy to help me breathe. That I may never walk out of that hospital. That I may have permanent brain damage due to poor oxygenation.

But our God had a different plan, and He created a miracle in a hopeless situation. The church had come together and people from all over were praying and believing for me to get better.

The doctor added that after getting much worse, all of a sudden (by God's grace!), I got a lot better. Only a few days later, they were miraculously able to extubate me. We talked more about the details, and she helped answer more of my questions.

But after she left the room to get back to work, I was filled with distress. All I could think about, over and over, was that Ava was intubated because of me. Because I got sick, she was intubated. She was all alone, scared, and her first day of life was marked by having a tube stuck down her tiny throat. I couldn't tuck that emotion away. It flooded over me. Weeping, alone in the room, I let the tears just roll down my face. I felt so guilty and ashamed. My little girl was alone, with no one to care for her…all because of me.

Aching, I had only a few moments to myself before the next nurse came in to give me my blood thinning shot and to check my vitals. I pulled myself together and smiled at her—because that's just what you do: put on a brave face. The walls in the room started to feel claustrophobic. I missed talking to people, and although the staff were treating me amazingly well, I missed having my family nearby. I called David but was too ashamed to tell him how guilty I felt about Ava, so I avoided the topic and we talked about his day and his plans.

Chapter Nine – Questions

This one was a deep one for me. I had so many reasons to feel guilty. As parents, we want only the best for our children, and I had to realize the reason I was feeling all this guilt.

It was more than just guilt, it was a failure to protect Ava from harm, failure to be there for her when she needed me most, and failure to comfort her. Identifying why I felt guilty was step one.

Not letting go of guilt will suffocate you, regardless of the severity of what you have done. It will not help you to keep holding on to guilt. If Jesus forgives us, the only one who benefits in keeping guilt is the enemy. He will rob you of who you can be, he will rob you of how you see yourself, and ultimately, he will rob you of living out your full potential.

It is important to remember that forgiveness may be a journey in itself. We might want to forgive others (or ourselves), but may find ourselves struggling to do so. It's not uncommon to need to rewire the way we feel and think. We need to continue to bring forgiveness to Jesus as certain emotions or memories come up. Do so until full freedom comes.

1.) Name your guilt and/or unforgiveness.

....

....

....

....

2.) Ask for forgiveness if it's appropriate.

....

....

....

....

3.) What does Jesus say about you and others?

....

....

....

....

4.) Forgive yourself and others continuously.

....

....

....

....

SCRIPTURES

1 John 3:20-22: "Even if we feel guilty, God is greater than our feelings and he knows everything. Dear friends, if we don't feel guilty we can come to God with bold confidence. And we can receive from him whatever we ask because we obey him and do the things that please him."

1 John 1:9: "But if we confess our sins to him, he is faithful and just to forgive us our sins and to cleanse us from all wickedness."

Psalm 51:9: "Don't keep looking at my sins. Remove the stain of my guilt."

Hebrews 10:22: "Let us go right into the presence of God with sincere hearts fully trusting him. For our guilty consciences have been sprinkled with Christ's blood to make us clean, and our bodies have been washed with pure water."

1 John 3:20: "Even if we feel guilty, God is greater than our feelings, and he knows everything."

Psalm 32:1: "Oh what joy for those whose disobedience is forgiven, whose sin is put out of sight."

1 John 1:10: "If we claim we have not sinned, we are calling God a liar and showing that his word has no place in our hearts."

Proverbs 28:13: "People who conceal their sins will not prosper, but if they confess and turn from them, they will receive mercy."

Psalm 32:2: "Yes what joy for those whose record the Lord has cleared of guilt, whose lives are lived in complete honesty."

TEN

My strength came in waves. I would get the feeling that I was OK so I would venture a walk from the bed to the window, but by the time I would get to the window, I was wiped out. I would sit for a few moments and then begin to feel OK again. I tried calling David but he didn't pick up, so I called a few friends. Even those FaceTime calls left me drained. Not only physically, but emotionally and mentally I was feeling so foggy, it was as if my mind couldn't clearly comprehend everything going on. At times, it felt as though I was on the outside looking in and observing.

Just then the physical therapist came in, and I quickly put on the charade of doing better than I actually was because of how desperately I wanted to go home. He asked me to walk back and forth across the room. I tried to pretend that I was able to walk effortlessly, hiding how truly difficult each step was for me. It was quite annoying that he kept on trying to talk to me while I was walking, because I couldn't walk and talk at the same time. My old expert-multitasker self would have been horrified! I was so focused on taking steps, I couldn't fathom putting together semi-coherent responses to his light conversation. I simply smiled at him, gesturing that I was not really able to adequately handle both those tasks at the same time. That's when he began to explain to me that my mind was actually still learning how to multitask and, at this point, I could only do one task at a time. It was so odd for my mind and body to have to relearn to do absolutely everything. Overall, I did very well and he seemed to be pleased with my progress. He mentioned that he had never seen anyone go from intubated to walking well in such a short period of time. That was an award in and of itself! My acting skills must have been stellar, and my determination was paying off.

During the night, I would have to wake up every two hours to pump. It was difficult to fall back asleep because the hospital bed was so uncomfortable after days of lying on it—plus, the oddest of feelings would come over me at night. It felt like I was jetlagged. I never thought about the fact that I would need to readjust to time as well. After being intubated for nine days, my mind and body had to relearn when it was day and night. I was so tired all day long but I couldn't fall asleep at night. I could hear every call light alarm going off and the nurses' voices, soft murmurs traveling down the empty hallways. I couldn't understand what they were saying, but the noise seemed to be just enough to keep me awake. Of course, when I would finally fall asleep, it was only to be awakened shortly thereafter for a vitals check. Then the alarm to pump and dump. So, the seemingly vicious cycle continued.

In the morning, the nurse came in to swab my nose to check if I was still Covid-positive. They shove that specimen stick up your nose till your brain feels it (metaphorically, of course), but still—*not* my favorite test. What felt like yet another long night was over, or so I thought to myself when I woke up at six o'clock. I figured I couldn't sleep anyway so I might as well stay up and get adjusted to earthly time.

I felt like Rapunzel—locked in her castle with food and clothing and no friends or family. The room was quite boring and there was little to do. I would get up and think about accomplishing something, maybe even something as simple as making my bed. I would get about halfway through when my hands would get super tired, the shortness of breath would kick in, and I would need to take a break. One long second after another—and then it was finally eight o'clock. David called, and I talked to him for a short while. I told him what the doctor said the previous day and that I wasn't sure how long I would have to stay here. Then David had to go, so I called a few other family members and friends and just lay around and waited. My food would come, but it smelled terrible and I had no appetite. My stomach was still very sensitive and would hurt anytime I would try to eat anything. The nausea was getting better, but the pain in my stomach and the rotten tomato smell in my nose kept my appetite to a minimum.

Most of my friends didn't really call or text. I think most people truly just didn't want to bother me. On the one hand, they were right. I didn't have the mental or physical capacity to carry real conversations with everyone. Yet a huge part of me wanted to bounce back to normal as quickly as possible. I wanted to have the energy and capacity I had before, to chat with my friends, to host, and to live life. Little did I know I was very, very far from normal.

At this point, I was taking only Tylenol, ibuprofen and my blood thinner shots. I didn't have any IVs attached and was no longer on any additional medications. I was treated like a princess with the plague. I had no contact with anyone, but had a nice, comfortable-enough room with a bed. People would come to my side if I needed anything.

During one of the FaceTime calls with David, he mentioned to me that Oksana had reached out to a few local news anchors in an effort to reach a large number of people and ask them to pray for me. I was so thankful to have prayer and had no clue what was waiting for me when I got home.

Early in the morning, a new doctor came in. I quickly sat up and was happy to see another human being. I gave him my full attention and, to my shock, he said, "I am here to discharge you."

Discharge! My heart pounded in my chest. "What? What does that mean? I thought I would be here for up to thirty days!" I exclaimed. He explained that because they were still figuring out this virus, there was no concrete protocol. He could keep me here at the hospital or I could go home and get better there. Of course, I said I wanted to go home! I missed David and Emily so much! I missed kissing David, the way it felt to have his arms embrace me, the way he smelled. I wanted to wrap my arms around Emily! I asked about Ava and he said that he had talked to the pediatrician, and that she needed to stay in the NICU because she was not yet able to eat well on her own. But I could go home! I couldn't believe it, just yesterday I thought I would have to be in the hospital for a month, and today I was getting sent home!

The doctor said he would start working on my discharge papers and I was simply overjoyed. Before I had time to process everything that had just been turned upside down in my life, one of my little brothers called. I asked him what he was doing and he responded with "nothing," adding that he had some time to kill before going to work. This is when I formed the perfect plan—I was going to surprise David! Finally, I was going to go home! This day felt like it would never come. I was ecstatic as I quickly packed up the few things I had: the pictures of my family that my coworkers had hung around the ICU room, Ava's tiny footprints and the clothing I had come to the hospital with. My heart was pounding and I realized I was pushing myself a little too hard. I was even starting to sweat just from getting my things together. I also had to change my postpartum pad and shed the hospital gown for my normal clothes. I started to feel nauseous and knew that if I didn't sit down, I would most likely pass out. So, I took a minute to catch my breath and steady the myriad of emotions racing inside of me.

The nurse came in a little bit after that and asked if I wanted to be wheeled out in a wheelchair. I said no, I would walk, but thankfully, she insisted and got one anyway. I finished packing my small bag of things and she came in with the wheelchair. I put on my face mask and sat down in the chair. As she wheeled me down the hospital hallways, with every step she took, I realized I could have only managed a fraction of those steps. I was up to being able to take about four steps before needing to stop and catch my breath. However, that was definitely not the time or place to admit that I was still feeling so crummy. I was so close to being home—*free*—and there was nothing that was going to stop me now! As I got near the hospital exit, I saw that some staff members had gathered to help celebrate my entrance back into the real world.

The ten-minute drive from the hospital to my house was truly the most beautiful ride I have ever taken. The wind was gently blowing and felt so refreshing; the sun was shining and warming my face and hands. The birds were singing and the trees were blooming. It was mid-April and spring beauty was just now starting to blossom everywhere. I was going home.

I had no clue that the hardest part of my journey was just about to begin.

CHAPTER TEN – QUESTIONS

When we overreact about something (explode) or underreact about something (numb our feelings), it's a good indicator that we need to deal with those emotions.

Here's a really practical way that I have been dealing with my emotions. This activity will take three steps:

1.) Identify your emotion.

....

....

....

....

2.) Identify the *why* behind your emotion.

....

....

....

....

3.) Identify the "Jesus thought" behind your emotion.

....

....

....

....

I start by writing down my emotion inside of a circle and then identifying why I'm feeling that way.

If I feel fear, I write "fear" in the middle of a circle. I then draw lines from the circle to identify the reasons I have fear, and put each of those reasons in circles (my children, finances, the economy, work, hurtful friendships, etc.)

Then, in each of those circles, I go even deeper into why I have fears in those areas. And finally, most importantly, I invite Jesus into the deepest, scariest fears. I have found that even in *those* fears, Jesus is still good. And I surrender to God my deepest fears. This can be applied to any emotion: anxiety, loneliness, anger, etc.

See example below.

ELEVEN

Pulling into the driveway, I instantly felt a sense of safety. This was home. Our property looked so full of light and life. I stepped out of the car and let the sun bathe me in warmth. It felt so good to be outside!

David was not home when we pulled in because he had made a run to Home Depot, so my brother Alex helped me out of the car, and into the house. It was *so* nice to be home. I looked around—the house was clean. It truly took all my energy, though, to just walk into the living room and sit down on the couch.

I was a little surprised and taken aback at how tired I felt from that short walk. I sunk helplessly into the couch. Alex and I talked while we waited for David to come home.

The next scene unfolded as if it was in slow motion. I saw David's truck pulling in and a deep anticipation arose within me. I was so happy and it felt so right that he was coming home.

David walked in. Our eyes met and in disbelief, he froze. "No way!" he exclaimed. "No way… no way… *no way…*" he continued to repeat as his eyes teared up. I slowly began walking toward him. Still wearing a mask, I was finally able to hug him. "No way" was all he could say for the next fifteen minutes. Finally, he was able to string more words together. He said he was canceling all his plans for the rest of the day. We proceeded to spend the day together—just us—for the first time in what felt like forever, face to face.

David helped me back to the couch and went off to shower.

Alex left, and it was just me and my husband at home. I wanted to shower, but had no strength to do that. Wanting so desperately to go back to normal, I insisted we go to my parents' house. I was so eager to see our older daughter, Emily. David insisted I should rest and that we could go see her tomorrow, but I felt so much guilt for not being with her for so long that I felt I couldn't *not* go see her. A part of me knew I should stay home, but I so desperately wanted to go and just be with family, to be near people. I had missed people and human interaction so much. To walk from the couch to the bedroom I needed to hold on to David, but that in no way deterred me from my plans. We got ready and drove out to my parents' house.

Still wearing a mask, I walked into my parents' home and was greeted with many tears and much love. My eleven-month-old Emmie seemed to have not skipped a beat; it felt as if I had never left her. She ran to me and hugged me, then proceeded to run off to her own little world. Surprisingly, she was walking quite well and playing all on her own. She wasn't even a year yet, but was running around like a two-year-old. Mom had been caring for her for almost four weeks now. I asked Mom if she could please watch her just a little while longer, as I knew there was no way I would be able to handle an energetic eleven-month-old. My mom was surprised that I would even ask. "There's no way I was going to let you have Emily back right now, after all you've been through," she said.

As we talked with my family, it dawned on me for the first time the amount of worry and stress my family had felt while I was sick in the hospital. I didn't even realize that my journey was not just *my* journey. My family would get together every single evening and pray for me. My parents and David were in constant communication about my care; they truly had to make some difficult decisions on my behalf. Every second someone was worried about me. I could see the heaviness in my mom's eyes. I gleaned that she was so happy at the moment, but that the weight she had carried for the past few weeks was catching up to her. She told me having Emily around was good for her—it was almost a distraction, and provided a way where she felt like she was helping me by caring for my daughter. I could tell she also had a shelf of emotions that she just kept packing away. As the days continued to pass, I realized more and more the heaviness of the weight that my family and friends had carried on my behalf.

I was so happy to be at Mom's house, but also entirely exhausted and drained of every drop of energy. David walked me to the car and we headed home. We got home and every step walking to the house pushed my limits. My legs were shaking, my lungs were burning and, to top it off, all I had been able to eat that day was applesauce. My mom had given me some soup but it smelled and tasted like rotten tomatoes to me. I remember asking David to make sure it was not rotten—it wasn't! It was simply my taste buds going crazy.

After we got home, David had to go to the pharmacy to pick up the blood thinner shots for me. I went to our room and sat down on the side of the bed. I desperately wanted to shower before bed, so very slowly I stepped into the shower. I turned on the refreshing warm water, feeling each drop on my face—and that is when the weakness finally got the best of me. I didn't have the strength to stand any more. I ended up sitting down on the shower floor, too weak to lift a hand, too weak to even form a word to call out for help. I simply sat on the floor, water rolling down my face and pain pulsing all through my body. It was as though every single muscle and fiber of my being was mad at me for pushing myself so hard.

I gathered all my strength and slowly got up. I couldn't bother with drying off or dressing myself. I only had enough strength to shuffle over to the bed, and still completely drenched, to lie down.

David came home and helped me get dressed. It was finally just the two of us. I wanted to kiss him so badly, but my Covid test had not come back yet, so I dutifully kept my mask on, lying down next to him. I couldn't believe we were finally reunited and it was my first night back home. I was so tired, but my mind kept racing. All the experiences and memories of the day kept flashing in my mind: seeing David, Emily and the rest of my family. Finally, my muscles relaxed just as the timer went off to pump and dump.

It took me a while, but I realized I just couldn't continue the effort of pumping my breast milk, only to have to toss it out. Having to pump every two hours while not eating anything but applesauce, still recovering from COVID-19 and being intubated, and on top of all that, healing from delivering a baby was just not realistic.

That day, I weighed myself and realized I had lost 40 pounds. I was too weak and was depriving my body of the much-needed rest it required to recover by having to wake up every two hours to pump. Later on, I ended up talking to my doctor and we both agreed that the best thing for my baby was a healthy mom. I was not in a place to continue pumping. I was so disappointed and wanted to press on and keep trying, but I knew I had no strength to do it.

That night, sleep eluded me again. I was physically drained, but my mind was energetic. And there it was, a tornado of emotions. I couldn't fall asleep. I just creepily stared at David. I couldn't believe that we were together again. I honestly don't know if I actually fell asleep or not. But morning finally came flooding into our room—Easter Sunday.

I'm not sure if it was because the medications had worn off or because I was keeping myself so busy, but almost all of my strength was gone. I needed help with every step I took. I was actually getting weaker after getting home, but refused to stop the pace I had started. I needed to—*had to*—see my Ava again.

Joyfully, I watched David get ready. He was so kind and gentle with me. He hugged me and was so patient as he watched me struggle to get dressed while trying to catch my breath.

On Easter Sunday we went to my parents' house for a family dinner gathering, with me keeping my mask on the entire time.

All my family had gathered and asked about my story. We spent the day thankful to God for sparing my life, thankful to the staff who cared for me, thankful to have such an amazing support system and thankful for every single person who prayed. Every time someone told me how much they prayed for me there was a small part of me that felt as though I was in debt to that person. All I could do was just say thank you, over and over again.

Shortly after coming to Mom's house, the pediatrician called me and let me know that my Covid test came back positive and that I was not going to be able to see Ava yet. He also told me that because I tested positive and David had been near me, he was also not able to see her anymore for the time being. We asked if anyone else from the family could visit since we as parents were not allowed, but they told us they had a strict "parents only" policy.

I was so heartbroken. The thought *I should have stayed at the hospital* kept circling in my head. I didn't know that my coming home would mean Ava would be left all alone. And that's when the wall holding back the emotions broke. I couldn't hold it in any longer. Fear, guilt, pain all came rushing in like a flood. I cried and cried. My family tried to comfort me, telling me that everything would be OK, "You'll see her soon" and "Be thankful for what you have". They were right, of course, but it did nothing to change what I was feeling at that moment. I made the decision to seek out a place where I could just grab a moment and simply talk to God. I didn't know what to say, so I just stood there, feeling guilty for even feeling sad. I knew God had saved my life and yet here I was, feeling melancholy and upset.

It was only a few days later that I finally realized I had never really understood the loving heart of God before. He wanted me to rest. He fully understood the hurt I was carrying. He was in no way mad at me for it. He was simply providing the time and space for me to go through true healing. Being the loving Father that He is, He afforded me the things that I didn't realize I needed, exactly when I needed them.

Over the next few months, my emotional healing began to take on a certain tone and character. Instead of shelving my emotions, as per usual, I would bring them to God, one by one. Not hiding anything. Not even knowing how to deal with them. I would pray and ask Him what His thoughts were. I would read my Bible and He would always faithfully answer me.

CHAPTER ELEVEN – QUESTIONS

Beautifully weak.

When we realize our strength is found when we are weak, it's so freeing. I needed to let go of all my deepest emotions, for I am strongest when I am resting in the arms of Jesus.

God is not scared of your biggest, ugliest emotions. He is able to handle it. He has not abandoned you.

1.) What is a pain you're too scared to invite Jesus into?

....

....

....

....

2.) Why are you scared to do so?

....

....

....

....

3.) What will happen if you continue to cope the way you have been coping?

....

....

....

....

4.) What will happen if you decide to change and face this emotion/memory/fear/pain?

…………………………………………………………………...

…………………………………………………………………..

…………………………………………………………………..

…………………………………………………………………...

5.) What does Jesus say about your emotion/memory/ fear/pain?

…………………………………………………………………...

…………………………………………………………………...

…………………………………………………………………...

…………………………………………………………………...

TWELVE

The following morning, I came to find out that there was a news reporter who had heard about my story and wanted to interview me. I honestly didn't have the strength or desire to do it, but there was a small voice inside of me that kept telling me, *maybe if my story can bring hope to somebody, then it would be worth sharing.* So, I made the decision to be vulnerable and to share my story on the news and social network platforms.

I did interviews on *Good Morning America, CBN, Dr. Oz, Fox News, The 700 Club* and many other news outlets and talk shows. Four days later, I was on the phone about an interview with *The Ellen Show* when I got the call from my doctor that my second Covid test came back negative. This meant that I would finally be able to see Ava! I was beyond excited. I told the producer I couldn't do the interview, and right then and there, I dropped everything that I was doing and prepared to meet my daughter.

Still being too weak and uncoordinated to drive, I asked David to drop me off at the hospital since they only allowed one visitor at a time. That day plays in slow motion in my head: walking to the elevator, riding up to the NICU, waiting to be let in, washing my hands and approaching her room. I could have sworn that I could hear my heart beating out of my chest. I could see her small head lying in the warmer... and then it was as if time stopped altogether. I slowly walked toward her, looking down at her precious, tiny face. So many emotions came flooding in at the same time. First, I was so amazed at her—every little detail of her face was absolute perfection. She was so much smaller in person than she seemed on the FaceTime video calls. Then out of nowhere, I was filled with a harsh wave of guilt. I slouched over her and started weeping. "I am *so* sorry baby, I'm so sorry that I have not been able to be here for you! That I have not been able to hold you while you're going through the hardest period of your life! That I was not able to cuddle with you. I'm sorry that I got sick and you were born early. But I'm here now, and I love you *sooo* much, my baby girl." I stood there, weeping over her for what felt like forever. All of a sudden, I was exhausted again. Just the act of standing for a few minutes was making me light-headed. With the help of some of the nurses, I was able to hold her. I sat down in the hospital chair, holding my tiny four-and-a-half-pound daughter. I was exhausted. Yet I couldn't figure out if I was emotionally or physically exhausted—probably both. I wanted to stay there longer, but I was so weak. Reluctantly, I had David come pick me up and we went back home. Later that afternoon, I went to visit Emily at my mom's house.

David did not feel comfortable with letting me drive, as I was still somewhat disoriented fairly often. So, he became the designated driver for all of my visits to see Ava at the hospital, to see Emily at my mom's house, and for everything else I needed to get done.

A few weeks later, we were finally able to bring Ava home. She had been in the NICU for a total of nineteen days. It had been absolutely heartbreaking to have our daughter away from us, all the while knowing that she needed help. Truthfully, though, I needed those nineteen days and they were good for me. It gave my body a chance to recover, however slightly. I would never have admitted it at the time, but not having to wake up every two hours to feed her was actually very good for my physical recovery. But emotionally, it ate away at me every day knowing that my daughter was in a hospital so far away from me. The reality was that as soon as she came home, I realized she was quite the difficult baby.

With Ava coming home from the hospital, I insisted that I wanted to have Emily home as well. I was so eager to reunite my family. Looking back, I definitely should've taken my mom's offer and allowed her to keep my older daughter for at least another month, but I was stubborn and determined to have my family back together, at any cost. I wanted to have things go back to "normal" as soon as possible.

Unfortunately, my new normal was way more than I could handle. Ava had a very, very sensitive stomach and we went through two different donor breast milks and seven different formulas. I tried chiropractic sessions, essential oils, heat packs and pretty much everything else to soothe my poor little one's tummy. Finally, after weeks and weeks of sleepless nights, I had a moment when I was lying in bed crying (per usual in those days), trying to be quiet so David wouldn't hear me, when I had a sudden thought cross my mind. *It would have been easier if I had just died.*

Mind you, everyone would come up to me and say, "Angela, I'm so glad you're doing so well, you're such a miracle," or "Your baby is such a miracle!" But the truth was, I was not doing well. In fact, I was really struggling. My mind, my emotions and the lack of sleep were all bringing me to a place of desperation. I did everything that I knew to do. I prayed, I fasted, I spoke life over myself, I did not pity myself at all, I did not focus on myself or my problems. Unfortunately, none of that was actually helping me process or heal. I was so busy trying to be OK that I didn't realize I needed to go back and simply acknowledge that I had a lot on my plate. One of my unhealthy coping mechanisms was to just keep going and keep being strong. What I didn't know then is that there is more beauty in being weak than we can ever imagine.

That night I decided to do the unthinkable. I invited God into my ugly emotions. I thanked God for saving my life, for saving Ava's life. But then I proceeded to share with Him everything—in the same way that I would have shared it with a close friend. I expressed how unfair it was that I didn't get to see Ava being born, that I didn't get to have the newborn cuddles or the chance to comfort my girl. I told Him how it broke my heart that I couldn't breastfeed her like I had planned. Even after months of trying, my milk supply simply dried up because I couldn't eat. I poured out that I was weak and scared. I admitted to Him how hard it was to keep up with this image of being a "miracle" who needed to have it all together. I told Him I was scared to disappoint Him or to say something wrong. I told Him every single detail of all the things I was too scared to share out loud with anyone else.

And somehow, verbalizing it all to Him, were the baby steps in my healing. I realized God doesn't want us to be strong. He encourages us to bring our burdens to Him. So, one by one, I felt God addressing each hurt that I had with His love.

I realized that it's OK to be weak, it's OK to ask for help. So, David and I hired a babysitter. She came in the mornings for a few hours, allowing me to sleep since I was not getting enough sleep at night. Slowly but surely, my joyful self started coming back—even if it was just glimpses at first. I would intentionally spend a few minutes every day watering the flowers (and not the weeds) in my life. Watering the good moments, the tiny victories.

The things that seemed so minimal that I would normally not notice—I would spend a few minutes every day pondering them. I would speak out what I was thankful for: "Ava slept an additional three minutes today" or "Emily didn't make a huge mess while eating." Every day, I would find something joyful, something good, something positive. I tried my best to not focus too much on the hardships.

This last year has brought me to a deep realization of what it means to be emotionally healthy. For me, it means the capacity of carrying a very heavy load with ease.

THIRTEEN

Even though I had been through so much trauma and Ava was still only sleeping a few hours a night, I desperately wanted to go back to my "normal" life, including returning to my job as a respiratory therapist.

My twelve-week maternity leave was quickly coming to an end. I called the maternity phone line and explained to them everything I had been through: that I was still intubated when Ava was born and had stayed hospitalized long after the beginning of my maternity. Still, they counted my twelve weeks of maternity leave starting from the moment Ava was born, regardless of the circumstances surrounding her birth. The lady on the phone sympathized with me, but rules were rules.

So, I went back to work in an on-call position twelve weeks later. I would work only one to two days a week. The thought of escaping my screaming newborn and fussy one-year-old sounded refreshing.

My first day was supposed to be a half-day: get my feet back into the department, freshen up on some of the medical devices, and go over the new Covid protocols. Little did I know, my first day back at work would look very different: I would end up visiting every department that I was sick in and have an overload of emotions.

While going over the new protocols, the department was short-staffed and needed an extra set of hands, so I agreed to help. One of the staff members called me asking if I could help in the labor and delivery unit because a woman was in labor and they were concerned for the baby's heart tones. I agreed and walked up to that floor, remembering how I walked the very same halls on my way to visit Ava. I came into the room and assisted with the birth. The respiratory therapist assigned to that unit was attending to another delivery that was happening at the same time. I remember watching the baby come and holding my breath as the baby started to cry, making sure everything was as it should be—no respiratory interventions required. I walked out of the room as my emotions began to bubble up inside again…but I pushed them down and kept walking. Further down the hall, some of the labor and delivery nurses stopped me and celebrated my recovery, expressing how happy they were to see that I was doing so well. I smiled and was thankful too, not wanting to admit to myself that as eager as I was to feel "normal", I really wasn't feeling normal at all.

When I got back to the respiratory therapists' office, a different therapist called me asking if I could help rotate a patient in the ICU, most likely not realizing that it was my first day back. Of course, I said I would help.

I walked down the hallway back to the unit where I fought for my life and my miracle happened.

As I walked through the doors of the ICU, many of the staff recognized me and came up to me; many of them I knew, some of them I didn't. Everyone celebrated my remarkable recovery. Many people told me they had prayed for me and I was showered with love. *Yes*, I thought, *I'm moving on, I got this*. So, I put on all of the required personal protective equipment and walked into the room to help rotate the patient. What I didn't realize was that I was walking into the exact room I was intubated in. While I was a patient in the ICU, I had no clue what room I was actually in.

The patient we were rotating was sick with Covid and on a ventilator. I walked in, helped, and then simply walked out, completely overwhelmed with emotions.

I was then asked if I could help with another patient's treatment. Of course, I agreed and walked up to the patient's room. Upon entering the room, I was faced with the same feelings I personally felt while I was a patient: the way it felt to be completely alone, to have no visitors. All of the emotions this elderly grandmother was feeling were filling me to the brim. I cared for her like I would for my own mom and went back to the department to do more computer work. About eight hours into the day, a coworker came up and jokingly said, "You know, they say you have immunity to Covid now, so I told them, why don't we throw Angela unmasked into an ICU Covid room and see what happens, ha-ha," he laughed.

A little taken aback, I couldn't get myself to laugh at his joke. "OK," I said passively, just to avoid the conversation. Finally, I was too overwhelmed to deal with any jokes or any more tasks so I told them I was ready to go home.

On my way home, I almost felt numb—emotions I thought I had already dealt with all came back unexpectedly. I didn't know how I should feel going back to work; I didn't know if it was OK for me to be anxious, or even what "normal" should feel like. Most of all, I didn't know how to react to all the staff members who prayed and cared for me. Do I thank them? Do I befriend them? I didn't know if it was OK to just do my job and leave. I felt like I was expected to be this shining star of health. But I was nowhere near my healthy previous self—not emotionally, not physically. I was still getting only a few hours of sleep a night and my body was still recovering. Going to work was hard, but staying home with two babies was hard too. It seemed that there was no escape from hardship.

Once again, I had to learn to deal with my emotions, but this time, they were old emotions that I had hoped I'd already healed from. Many of my coworkers shared how hard it was for them to see me so sick, and how much stress it had put on them. They would say things like "You have no clue what you put us through," again filling me with an odd sense of guilt. I was so sorry. I wanted to help them heal as well, but wasn't sure how to respond. Most days, I would simply say, "I'm so sorry, tell me about it, how are you doing now?", trying to help them emotionally. I had to learn to navigate the social pressure of everyone recognizing me and dealing with the emotional flashbacks. I had to slowly ask myself hard questions, trying to pinpoint the emotions I was feeling. It took months and months of healing until I was able to go to work and not feel anxious.

I would feel thankful, but kind of like I owed something to each person who told me they prayed for me. Naturally, I'm more of a private person, so it was hard for me to have strangers recognize me. I had to learn how to navigate comments that people made about my health or jokes that were hurtful to me. I had to relearn what it meant to have a normal life.

Ultimately, I realized this experience forever changed me: my life would never be the same again.

Throughout this past year, I had to learn to go back to life: to learn to juggle being a mom of two, a wife and handle all the uncertainties of life. It's certainly been the hardest year of my life. It was hard on my marriage. It was hard on my daughters. It was hard on my family. Yet, I am a much stronger person now after overcoming my greatest challenges and experiencing my greatest miracles.

I had to understand the stress David was experiencing. I had to learn and work daily to find grace for others (and myself). I had to learn to be a good wife, mom, sister and person, and to strive for emotional health every day. But the most amazing thing is that we are *not* in this world alone—we have hope, we have Jesus, and ultimately every situation in our life should bring us closer to God and closer to His truth about who we are.

Regardless of all the hardships we face, we are not defined by our circumstances. Your hardship could lead you to one day being the healthiest version of yourself. I realized that striving for my old "normal" would never bring me happiness in my current reality. That "normal" will never be the "normal" in my life again.

I ended up quitting my job and staying home as a full-time mom. Doing so forced me to reevaluate my worth and even my identity. I loved working so much. I loved my job, my coworkers, and what I did as a profession. I graduated with honors from my respiratory care program; I specialized in pediatric and neonatal respiratory care. I was pursuing my dream job. Going to work left me satisfied knowing that I was contributing to society in a significant way. I would drive home stressed and exhausted but satisfied, knowing that I had literally helped save a life that day.

One day, I hope to go back to work. But in the meantime, my new normal is not Angela, the respiratory therapist. It's Angela—the mom, the wife, the friend and the daughter. The achievements I held on to so dearly I had to let go of. Having to let go of all of that, even for just a season, forced me to rediscover myself outside of my career. And for me, that was not easy. It was so difficult to feel important when caring for my children daily—that did not give me the instant gratification that work did. Work came with its own set of challenges, but staying home with the kids was also difficult.

Thankfully, throughout this year, I have been able to re-identify what success looks like to me. I was not successful just because I had an amazing job and a career and was able to "do it all". It is amazing when people have goals and achieve them, however more important than any goal is *how* we are living. A successful life is when we can love well. When I can treat my family, children, and spouse with love. When I can put others first. When my life is an image of what it means to *be in love*. Whether I'm at work or at home, do I love well? It's been bittersweet having to take a break from my career, but in the meantime, I am learning to embrace this season.

This new season is one where *everyone's* "normal" is no longer "normal." I want to challenge you, dear reader, to let go of your old "normal" and learn to live in this current reality. There's so much uncertainty, but the reality is, we may never go back to the old normal, and what we have left is our current reality. So, let's make the best of it. Let's disagree with love, let's live with love, let's do everything filtered through the lens of love. And then, maybe, just maybe, our new reality, however different it may be, could be a reality where we live full of love and full of hope.